Contents

CONTENTS

Preface

Neat handwriting, a pencil and a rubber. Twenty years ago, when the first edition of this book appeared, these were considered the key requirements for an efficient hotel receptionist. Today the key requirements are more complex, take longer to learn and have a far greater impact upon profit. A good receptionist can easily add thousands of pounds to the profit of a hotel by being positive about sales and professional about filling the last room.

This major re-write of *Front Office Operations* covers the reality of hotel work as we cross into a new century, but still covers the timeless systems and procedures that underpin the work of hotel reception desks around the world.

Colin Dix

CHAPTER 1

The Hospitality Industry and the Hotel Reception

After studying this chapter you should be able to

- outline the important aspects of the hospitality industry
- describe the main forms of ownership of hotels
- explain the different organisation structures of small, medium and large hotels
- define the roles and responsibilities of the hotel receptionist in each
- outline how the rooms division is organised in a large hotel, and the main tasks of the employees

The hospitality industry

The term 'hospitality' has become accepted over the years as a generic word which describes all the activities that relate to services and facilities for tourists and travellers. The hospitality industry is a major contributor to the national economy and to the generation of employment, with a potential for future growth that cannot be rivalled elsewhere. The growth of the industry is tied to demand, and this continues to increase. The demand is wide and varied, with all types of individuals looking for all manner of different services.

Hospitality providers include

- hotels
- restaurants
- travel and transport
- theatres
- leisure centres
- information centres
- visitor attractions
- heritage sites
- theme parks

and many more. Many of the sectors are sponsored by government departments, so the industry is a rare combination of the public and private sectors. Even the public sector needs to be profit-motivated now, and many billions of pounds are returned to the national economy each year.

The hotel sector

The hotel sector represents a vital part of the hospitality industry since the provision of accommodation, food and beverage is essential for anyone spending time away from home, whether it be for business or pleasure.

As the nature of the traveller will vary, so the category of hotel available to them will differ accordingly. The star rating system in the UK is the subject of much debate. There is a great deal of confusion, particularly for those based overseas, since a number of different organisations rate hotels, and the criteria are not always the same. As long ago as 1963 a proposal was made that there should be a grading system on an international basis, but it is still a vision of the future. Some advance has at least been made in the UK and the AA, RAC and ETB have produced detailed proposals for classification by a harmonised star rating system.

Whether a system awards stars, flags, crowns or rosettes, the general principle is to grade the hotel in such a way that the clients will have a benchmark against which they can compare the service on offer with the price that is quoted.

The star rating system is based upon the facilities that the hotel offers, and the service it provides. This may be as basic as a room with breakfast, or as sophisticated as the service offered in a luxury five-star operation (Fig. 1.1). The facilities offered by a hotel of this nature may include most, or all, of the following:

- room/bathroom en suite
- 24-hour service in all departments
- radio, TV and video in rooms
- fax/modem
- several restaurants
- lounge(s)
- cocktail bar
- public bar
- room service
- meetings and conference rooms
- banqueting facilities
- valet service
- health club, sauna and gym
- pool
- cinema
- entertainment
- garaging
- concessions – shops let as kiosks, hairdressers, etc.

The decision to stay in a particular hotel may be influenced by various factors. One factor will certainly be the price. The guest will also be influenced by other variables, such as the facilities on offer, the location, or the size.

Fig. 1.1 *Luxury hotels provide a variety of services and facilities.*

Many guests have an affinity with a particular group or chain of hotels and always seek out an establishment in which they feel the surroundings are familiar. A chain of hotels generally refers to a number of operations that belong to the same organisation.

International corporate hotels

These are large chains which are almost household words in the hotel and catering industry (e.g. Hilton, Holiday Inns, Inter-Continental, Marriott). Some of the groups are a combination of company-owned, franchised and management contract operations, while others are entirely owned by an individual or a company. Their main features include standardisation of service, facilities and price, and many chains endeavour to operate a hotel in most major capitals in the world, and many of the provincial towns also.

Major national hotel companies

The UK has its share of international hotels and many of our major national hotel companies are equally well known abroad. This sector of the trade is increasingly dominated by the breweries, who have expanded into the hotel business over the last few years.

Fig. 1.2 *The Holiday Inn, Garden Court, Nottingham. An international corporate hotel.*

Small hotel groups

Not all groups of hotels are large or widely dispersed. Some companies own a group that may consist of no more than four or five hotels, and they may be confined to a particular area such as the Lake District or the South Coast.

Independent hotels

These are units which are privately owned or independent of any company. Many guests enjoy staying at an establishment of this nature because of the individuality of the operation. The disadvantage is, of course, that when staying in other towns or countries the guest must find another hotel which suits them and caters for their needs.

Hotel consortium

This system overcomes the disadvantage referred to above since it provides a way for independently owned hotels to affiliate themselves to one another without surrendering their individuality. The advantages to the hotel include shared advertising costs, bulk purchasing and a referral of bookings, and to the guest a standardising of quality.

Fig. 1.3   *The Lindrick Hotel. Independent privately owned.*

Organisation structures

Hotels come in all shapes and sizes, but generally can be categorised into

- small
- medium
- large

Deciding which category a hotel falls into may be quite difficult. Who decides when a small hotel becomes medium? Generally it is quite subjective, because we base our decision on our own experience. If you have never worked in a hotel larger than 20 bedrooms, then 50 can seem very large. If, on the other hand, you have never worked in anything smaller than 500 bedrooms, 50 is very small indeed.

As a rough guide, in the UK the sizes shown in Fig. 1.4 (overleaf) are generally agreed.

Often it is not the size of the hotel that governs its systems, but the category. Many luxury hotels operate the same types of systems, but can vary in size enormously. Over the last decade a number of hotels have opened which follow the American system, and provide a good, standard service, but with few additional services. These hotels may be quite large, but the staffing structure will be minimal compared to traditional hotels providing all the services.

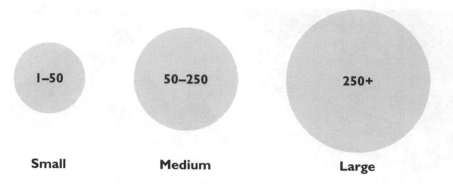

Fig. 1.4 *Hotels in the UK.*

As a general rule of thumb, the job of the receptionist will be more varied in the smaller and medium hotels, than in the larger ones. The larger the operation, the greater the likelihood of there being specialist roles, so front office might be divided into reception, advance reservations and cashier. In a smaller operation the same person would perform all these functions, and often operate the switchboard as well.

Clearly, for training purposes a small or medium hotel is a good starting point, since there is an opportunity to see the whole job through from beginning to end.

Reception in the hotel organisation

As hotels vary in size, shape and age, so the exact role of the reception department will differ from one hotel to another. The majority of hotels earn the bulk of their revenue and profits from the sale of rooms, so it is essential that the reception department is organised and staffed to maximise sales. Guests, whether staying in a 600-room airport hotel or a small country inn with six rooms, invariably approach the reception desk for information, assistance and answers to any problems they encounter in the hotel.

Small hotels

In a small hotel the reception will have a number of tasks to carry out. In addition to checking in guests, they will have to act as secretary and telephonist. A typical organisation structure is shown in Fig. 1.5. In this type of hotel it is probable that all staff members will carry out a variety of jobs: the restaurant waiters will serve in the lounge, and perhaps deliver room service orders, and the manager will probably be responsible for banking, stocktaking, food purchasing and other tasks that would merit separate departments in a larger hotel.

Fig. 1.5 *Organisation structure of a small hotel.*

The assistant manager is unlikely to have a clearly defined responsibility for any area. Normally, in the absence of the general manager the assistant will deputise by carrying out the work. When both are on duty the assistant will be allocated tasks on an *ad hoc* basis by the manager.

Medium hotels

As the hotel becomes larger, so it is possible to organise it into more clearly defined departments, each with a departmental head. Figure 1.6 shows the organisation structure of a medium-sized hotel. The size of the hotel, and the length of time that services are open, will mean that more staff are required here than in a small hotel. This is also true of management personnel. In a small hotel we have seen that there will be a manager with one assistant. In the medium hotel the post of assistant manager will probably be held by two people. These two assistants will work alternate shifts so that management supervision is provided from 0800 to 2300 hours, seven days a week. One assistant will work from 0800 to 1600 hours, while the other will cover the evening shift from 1600 to 2300 hours. The duties of an assistant manager will vary from one hotel to another, but it is rare for the assistant manager to have any specific duties apart from management supervision.

Fig. 1.6 *Organisation structure of a medium-sized hotel.*

If the department heads have a problem, or require assistance, they approach the assistant manager who is on duty at the time. It can be seen from Fig. 1.6 that all departments are independent of each other, with each department head reporting directly to management. This organisation structure encourages departments to be insular and to think only of their own needs, therefore if there is a dispute it is often the guests who suffer: their needs are not considered at all.

Large hotels

With large hotels of more than 250–300 rooms it is easier for greater specialisation to occur. This type of hotel can afford to use the skills of full-time accountants, security officers and personnel managers. Naturally, this means there is a greater level of professionalism in the different departments and sections of the hotel. Figure 1.7 shows the management team of a large hotel. The revenue-earning areas of the hotel are split into two main divisions: **Food and Beverage** and **Rooms Division**.

The managers of these two divisions are members of the management team of the hotel (along with the accountant and other specialists) but obviously they will be responsible for a greater number of people than the other managers.

The management team represents the operating functions of the hotel and is responsible for co-ordinating the various activities that are necessary to the smooth running of a large business. They will work together to organise complex conferences or large package tours that will use the hotel's facilities.

The management team will also carry out the executive functions of the hotel – setting budgets, sales plans, and operating systems will be included in their responsibility. It is common for members of the management team of a large

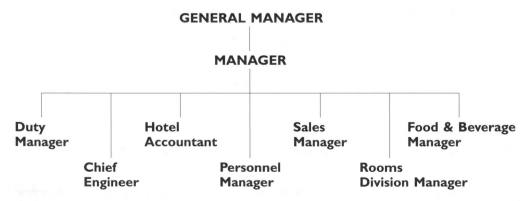

Fig. 1.7 *Organisation structure of a large hotel.*

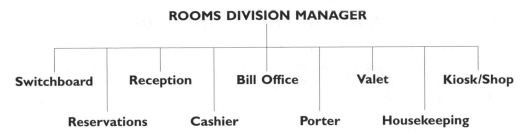

Fig. 1.8 *Organisation structure of rooms division in a large hotel.*

hotel of this type to earn more than the manager of a small hotel, for they will be responsible for a larger staff and a far greater turnover.

Figure 1.8 shows how the rooms division is organised. Co-ordination with other sections of the hotel is achieved by the rooms division manager, who is part of the management team. He or she is totally responsible for the co-ordination of the individual departments under their control. All the departments shown in Fig. 1.8 have to work together to make the guest's stay enjoyable and to see that the functions of the rooms division are smoothly carried out. This system of organisation clearly puts the needs of the guest first; consequently there are fewer disputes between the individual departments. The hotel is organised around the needs of the guest. This is very different from the hotel where the guests feel that they are merely an irritation to be pushed around from one department to another by staff members who say very curtly, 'It's not my job.'

The task of the assistant manager in a large hotel is very different from that carried out in a smaller unit. The job title is often 'duty manager', and the main responsibility is dealing with guests. The job is to get problems solved and deal with complaints and queries. But the duty managers are without line authority: they have to resolve the problem through the appropriate member of the management team, or, in their absence, with the department head or supervisor on duty. Duty managers will cover a rota of 24 hours: so for the guest there is always a member of management available to deal with problems. Often the guest is not aware that they are dealing with a relatively junior member of the management of the hotel, for the duty manager will be an expert at dealing with people and handling complaints.

The general manager in hotels of this size may never see a guest from one week to the next. The job is similar to that of a senior industrial manager; they are responsible for policy, long-term planning and co-ordination of the whole business.

The departments in rooms division

This section will outline the various tasks and responsibilities of the departments that go together to make up the rooms division. Only the largest hotel will have all of these different departments, and in many small units many of them will be amalgamated.

Hours and shifts

Large hotels really do never close. They have to operate 24 hours a day, 365 days a year. But obviously not every department will operate at full strength all the time. Night duty is from 2300 to 0800 hours and a separate night staff will be employed to work these hours. Day staff will work either early (0800 to 1600 hours) or late (1600 to 2300 hours) and sometimes cover night duty when a permanent member of the night staff is off duty, or on holiday. There is usually at least a half-hour 'handover', when both shifts are there together.

Naturally, accounts, personnel and other 'office' departments will operate during normal office hours. Figure 1.9 shows how a 24-hour coverage of the main departments is provided by key departments, so a restricted service is available even at night for all the rooms division functions. This would also be the case in the food and beverage department.

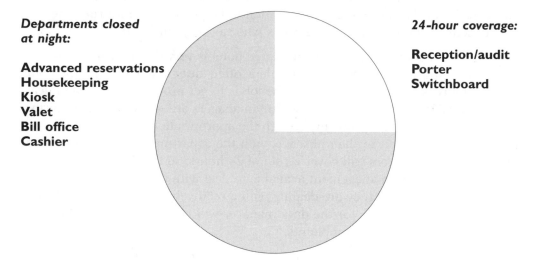

Departments closed at night:

Advanced reservations
Housekeeping
Kiosk
Valet
Bill office
Cashier

24-hour coverage:

Reception/audit
Porter
Switchboard

Fig. 1.9 *Twenty-four-hour coverage of rooms division in a large hotel.*

Telephones

The advance of automation is most apparent in the telephone department of large hotels. The number of telephone staff per 100 guests has never been lower. Facilities that can now be carried out without the assistance of an operator include world-wide dialling from the guest room, automatic recording of the charge in the bill office, an automatic early-call system and a message-taking system. The introduction of these facilities has vastly improved the service in most hotels.

As the switchboard is staffed 24 hours a day, it is also the location of the fire-checking equipment.

Advance reservations

Most bookings will be taken by the advance reservations department. This is normally located near the reception desk, but is not in view of the guests. This department is usually staffed from 0800 to 1800 hours as most reservation requests are received during working hours, with peaks around 1000 and 1500 hours for telephone bookings. Naturally, reservations will still be received when staff are off duty, but faxes will be dealt with the next day, and telephone calls are usually taken by reception.

Reservation office staff must have a clear speaking voice, but their appearance and dress do not matter so much, for they do not come into direct contact with the guests. Many hotels use the advance reservations department as a training ground for people wishing to work in reception.

Reception

Twenty-four-hour coverage will be provided by the reception desk, but in large hotels the duties are specialised. Checking in guests and allocating rooms is their main responsibility. Additionally, they will answer queries from guests, and take reservation requests over the counter. Much of the work involves acting as an information clerk, either answering guests' questions directly, or referring them to the appropriate department of the hotel.

Cashier

Accepting payment of guests' bills and dealing with currency exchanges are the major tasks of the cashier. The safe-deposit boxes for guests' valuables will also be located in the office. Other sales departments of the hotel will receive their floats and pay in their takings at the cashier's office. The head cashier may prepare the banking and carry out the paying-in to the bank, but in some units this will be done by a member of the accounts staff.

Night coverage between 2300 and 0800 hours is given by a night auditor who will also post charges to update client accounts, produce a trial balance and prepare management reports. The float with which cashiers may start a shift will probably be in excess of £500, so it is essential that they are familiar with money and confident in handling very large sums. Honesty is the prime qualification for the job and most cashiers will be 'bonded' with an insurance company so that the hotel is covered against a dishonest act by one of the cashiers.

Bill office

This department, like advance reservations, is not a direct guest contact one. Also, like advance reservations and reception, it is often used as a proving ground for people who will later act as cashier. The main task is the posting of charges and payments on to guests' bills and extracting summaries of sales figures. Clearly, bill office staff need to be methodical in their working habits and have a grasp of figures, even though much of the work is carried out on computers or accounting machines and calculators.

Porters

'Concierge' is the French term for porter and it often appears over the desk in luxury hotels, but not every porter comes into this category. Some units separate the department into two, with an enquiry desk and luggage porters. The head porter (or concierge) is traditionally a person of high status in the hierarchy of the hotel, responsible for guest keys, enquiries, mail, theatre tickets, car hire, baggage and other guest services. Recently, however, many of these tasks have been removed and concessions rented to specialist ticket agencies and car hire companies. Some tourist hotels do not have a head porter at all; instead there is an enquiries desk and luggage handling is supervised from the reception.

Valet

Dry cleaning, pressing and guest laundry are handled by the valet, who reports to the head housekeeper. The job is now only found in the most expensive hotels, as many guests are more than willing to wash small items of clothing in the bathroom and borrow an ironing board from the housekeeper.

Kiosk

A shop in the lobby of the hotel will either be operated directly by the hotel, or, more commonly, be rented out as a concession to a specialist company. It will sell newspapers, gifts, tobacco and other useful articles. In the concession agreement the hotel will have the right to dictate important points concerning opening hours and the range of goods on sale. They may insist, for example, that the kiosk sells toothbrushes and toilet articles as a service to guests. They may equally refuse permission for some things to be sold, believing that it would not fit the image of the hotel.

Housekeeping

Numerically, this is the largest department in the hotel, because one maid is needed for every 12–15 rooms. The housekeeper is responsible for the preparation of guest rooms for sale and the cleanliness of all public areas of the hotel. Close liaison between the housekeeper and reception is essential so that rooms are available to let as quickly as possible. Requests for extra blankets or other services are often passed to housekeeping through the reception department. Most housekeeping staff will work between 0800 and 1600 hours although some maids and a supervisor will be on duty during the evening until 2300 hours to service the rooms of late departures, carry out cleaning duties, and possibly turn down beds. In some transient hotels, 24-hour servicing is provided by the housekeeping department. Increasingly many hotels have come to rely upon the services of contract cleaning, rather than employing a full staff on the payroll. Whether the job is done in-house or contracted out, it is still a vital service, and one on which the hotel will ultimately be judged.

All of these departments will have a department head or supervisor who will report to the rooms division manager.

The cashier and bill office staff report to the hotel accountant for matters of operating procedure, training and policy but they are responsible to the rooms manager for their shifts, appearance, and supervision in day-to-day matters. This split responsibility requires a good working relationship between the rooms manager and the hotel accountant so that there is no conflict in the instructions that are given to the operating staff of the departments.

Career opportunities

The hotel and catering industry has always been renowned for the variety of opportunities that it presents, but recent developments have ensured that today's employees may work in many different settings, doing varied jobs and using a variety of skills.

Most colleges now recognise that a receptionist must have an awareness of the functions of the other areas of the hotel, and many courses now ensure that the front office is seen as part of the whole of the hotel, rather than an isolated section. Most college-leavers now have the opportunity to ensure that they are also proficient in many related skills.

Other sectors of the catering and leisure industry where front office staff may seek employment include the following outlets:

- restaurants – traditional or fast food
- wine or cocktail bars
- public houses
- clubs – traditional members' clubs or night clubs
- transport catering – flight, ships or trains
- conference centres
- leisure centres

Regardless of the countless opportunities which exist for front office staff, for most employees the main decision that they will make regarding future employment will be related to the size of the hotel.

The best-qualified staff will have some experience in both large and small hotels, but a typical career path in front office is shown in Fig. 1.10.

Professional and technical associations

Most qualified staff will be concerned to protect their own professionalism, and the hotel and catering industry is no exception. A variety of associations are in existence, far too numerous to name, but most can be classified into types according to their aims and objectives.

The associations seek to achieve and maintain professional standards by examining the skills of students and employees, and include the following:

C & G	City and Guilds
EdExcel	Educational Excellence
HCIMA	Hotel and Catering International Management Association

Other associations may represent a voluntary organisation of people who share the same occupational skills, and wish to see the advancement of their mutual interests:

| Clefs D'Or | Organisation of Head Hall Porters |
| Guild of Sommeliers | Organisation of Wine Waiters |

Another association of importance in the hotel and catering industry is concerned with the supervising, encouraging and carrying out of vocational training – not only for young people about to enter the industry, but also for those who wish to change their career, or those who wish to further it by taking supervisory courses. The HtF (Hospitality Training Foundation) fulfils all of these functions.

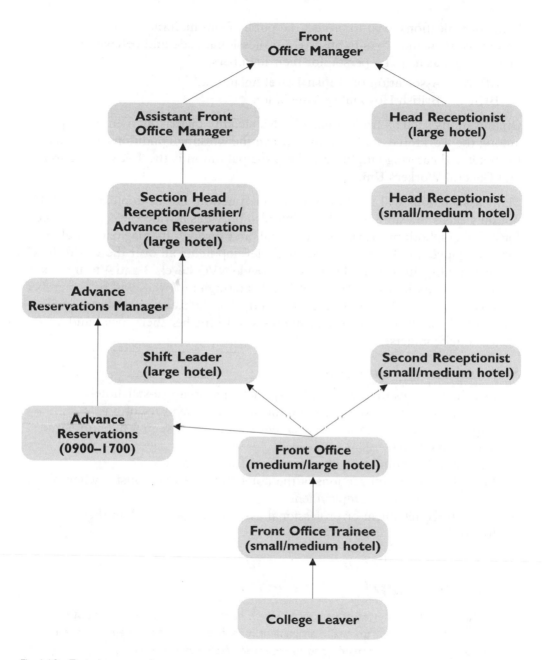

Fig. 1.10 *Typical career paths.*

Some organisations exist to protect the public from malpractice and to encourage their members to observe a professional code and behaviour, they may also act as a spokesperson for their members:

ABTA   Association of British Travel Agents Ltd
BHA   British Hospitality Association

Organisations such as trade unions have a steadily increasing membership among the workforce, and seek to improve the working conditions and payment for hotel and catering employees. The principal union is the T & G (Transport and General Workers Union).

Many associations will fulfil more than one function. For example, the HCIMA not only seeks to examine students, but also provides a wide variety of services for members, both professional and social, and through its magazine enables many employees to keep up to date with developments all over the world. It is in partnership with City and Guilds to provide NVQ Levels 3 and 4 to members of the hospitality industry. Most hotel and catering employees will be a member of at least one association or organisation during their career, and some will join several, either to protect their interests or to further their social and professional contacts.

Self-assessment questions

1 List the facilities that you would expect to find in a five-star hotel.
2 Give the main types of ownership for different categories of hotels.
3 Explain the difference in management structure between a medium-sized and a large hotel.
4 What are the main tasks of a receptionist in a small hotel?
5 List other important sections of the hotel and catering industry where front office staff may gain employment.
6 Name three technical or professional associations and explain their function.

Assignment

A hotel has had a series of walk-outs, which have become the main topic of conversation at departmental management meetings. The most recent has been investigated fairly thoroughly, and the following facts have emerged.

The clients – a couple and three children – checked in one evening at around 2200 hours. They were chance bookings, but the receptionist took a deposit for the first night's accommodation and tax.

When the morning shift arrived they entered the booking onto the computer, since it had not been done the night before. At 1400 hours the housekeeper reported that they had not vacated the room, so a message was left on the system for them to call reception. The hotel was not full, so it was not really a problem. When the family arrived back in, they called reception, and said they wanted to stay until the weekend, so their stay was extended, and all the departments were advised of the departure date. The hall porter reported that they had been very friendly, had been on several trips, and always appeared very pleasant. The restaurant staff said they always added a tip when they signed the bill, and most staff were eager to serve them. The housekeeper said the room was usually quite tidy, although they had very little luggage for a relatively large family, who were staying (she was told) until the end of the month. In public relations they were anxious to please this family, since he worked for a well-known company, whose business would be a great asset to the hotel if they could get this client to recommend them. The barman reported that, 'The gentleman liked a drink, but never brought the children down. He usually sent them and his wife something upstairs and put it on the bill.'

By the time the family walked out they had accumulated a large bill and several different stories had grown up around them.

Tasks

1 List the departments that were at fault in this scenario.
2 Write a report for the general manager explaining how this could have happened.
3 List the departments that were not involved but should have been.
4 Outline ways in which this situation could be avoided again.

CHAPTER 2

Care of the Customers

After studying this chapter you should be able to

- list the main security provisions in place in hotels
- state the practices that will contribute to health and safety in the workplace
- outline the main principles of fire prevention
- explain the importance of customer care and satisfaction
- describe the roles, responsibilities and main attributes of a receptionist
- state the areas of co-operation between departments

Hotel security

Everybody likes to work in a safe and secure environment, and there are many ways in which the reception staff can contribute to this. Several factors will influence the general security of the hotel, and many of them are controlled by the reception staff. Virtually all hotels will have recognised policies and at the very least security measures will be in place around the following:

- keys
- lost and found property
- equipment
- safety deposits
- cash handling
- guest arrivals
- guest check-out
- security incidents

At this point it may be useful to examine some common policies relating to these important security areas.

Keys

Submasters and masters

The management is usually quite careful about the allocation of submaster and master keys, since they will open all the rooms on a floor or in a block, or in the case of the master, all the rooms in the hotel which are not subject to a special lock. Usually masters are given only to heads of departments, and submasters are often signed in and out at the beginning and the end of a shift. To lose one of these keys is regarded as a very serious offence, since if the hotel wants to be really safe there is no alternative other than to change all the locks – even in a small hotel this would cost many thousands of pounds.

Room keys

Once the guest is given the key to the room it shows that the check-in process is nearly complete.

Some hotels have a traditional key, often fastened to a large ring or tab (Fig. 2.1). This is to remind the guest to hand in the key when they go out, and on departure. Sometimes this does not work, and the guest takes the key away, which poses a big problem for the hotel, since if that client is still in possession of the key, they can easily get back into the room. Clearly this becomes a problem once that room has been re-let to another guest. Additionally, keys need to be stored somewhere safe, where guests cannot see who is in or out, and in a large hotel this can be quite a task (Fig. 2.2).

Fig. 2.1 *A traditional room key.*

Fig. 2.2   *Room keys need to be stored out of sight of guests.*

One way of improving security with this type of system is by issuing clients with something that they can use to identify themselves to the staff in the hotel.

A key card

Some hotels give a key card to their guests when they check in. This is either a card or a small booklet which has the guest's name, room number and room rate entered on it. Inside or on the reverse there are details of the restaurants or other facilities of the hotel. Sometimes this is linked to advertising for local shops and it may then be self-financing (Fig. 2.3, overleaf). Key cards can be printed in different colours to indicate the different status of guests: a red card, for example, may indicate a chance guest, who could therefore be asked to pay cash for all services. A key card fulfils three separate functions:

- it can be used a security check when guests collect their keys;
- it can advertise facilities, both in and out of the hotel;
- it satisfies the hotel's legal obligation to inform guests of their room rate.

If the hotel procedure is to check the key card of the guest before charging anything to the account, or before handing over the key, then some fraud may be prevented, but there will always be a few genuine cases when a client may not be able to produce a key card: there may be two or more people in the

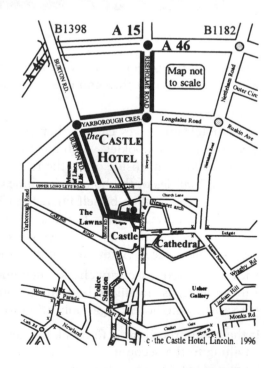

Fig. 2.3   *A key card can fulfil a number of functions.*

room, or they may have left the key card in the room. If this happens it is important to avoid upsetting the client, yet still follow the security procedures.

Many hotels have overcome these problems through the use of new technology.

Electronic key systems

Electronic key systems replace the traditional systems, and are far more secure both for the hotel and for the client. The keys are made of plastic and resemble a credit card. They are printed for each new arrival, with a combination number exclusive for that particular stay; masters and submasters are treated in the same way. If a key is lost or stolen it is a simple matter to re-program the lock, and then any existing key becomes worthless. The keys can also be used for authorisation and direct debiting in the restaurant, bars and other sales areas of the hotel, and this eliminates the risk of charges being posted to the wrong bill. When linked with a cash register that has preset pricing for each item, the system becomes almost foolproof. Some hotels also use the key as a trigger for the lighting and air-conditioning, so that without the key neither of these services will operate. Clearly this is a cost saving for the hotel, since many guests are careless about the costs of services (Fig. 2.4).

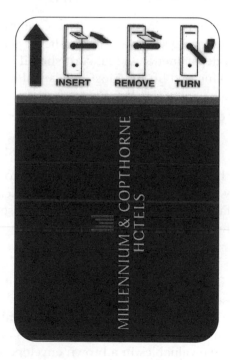

Fig. 2.4 *An electronic key system is more secure.*

Lost and found property

All lost and found property should be treated in the same way:

- held in a secure place
- reported to the supervisor
- recorded in the book
- returned to the owner if possible

In the case of more valuable items, additional security measures need to be in force. In the case of items such as passports, every effort needs to be made to find the client – usually at the airport!

Items which are found that come into the category of suspicious items must be treated with great care:

- their presence should be reported to security or management;
- they must not be touched or moved;
- they should be identified only if it is safe to do so.

In extreme cases, a decision may be taken to evacuate the area, and the reception staff should remain vigilant and observant at all times to protect the staff and customers of the hotel.

Equipment

All areas of the hotel use some form of specialised equipment, and the care of equipment will vary from one department to another. There are several factors that are common to all departments and all staff should be aware of the techniques of safe handling and lifting. Most hotels will have some form of policy relating to the following:

- prevention of loss or damage
- misuse
- cost-effective usage
- crime prevention
- risk analysis
- hazard reduction

Clearly some areas of the hotel will benefit much more from risk analysis and hazard reduction study than the reception area, but a quick look around most offices will produce a fairly lengthy list, ranging from loose floor tiles to badly positioned cups of coffee.

Safety deposits

Hotels are obliged to offer guests safety-deposit facilities if they wish to limit their liability for loss (see Chapter 3). A range of methods are available, often depending upon the size of the hotel, and the type of clientele. The most basic of systems, often used in smaller establishments, centres around the hotel safe and relies upon storing the valuables in a brown envelope or similar container.

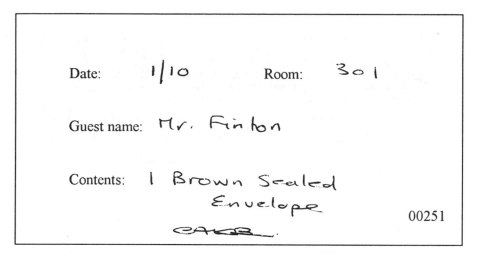

Date: 1/10   Room: 301

Guest name: Mr. Finton

Contents: 1 Brown Sealed
Envelope
00251
~~CASH~~.

Fig. 2.5   A safe-deposit two-part receipt.

Deposit envelope

The guest is offered a strong envelope into which they seal their property and sign over the seal. The cashier marks the envelope with the guest's name and room number, and issues a receipt for the envelope. The receipt is countersigned by the guest and the receipt number is noted on the envelope, which is deposited in the safe with other property. The receipt is issued for a 'sealed envelope'. By doing this, the cashier is relieved of the task of counting sums of money, or agreeing an inventory of contents with the guest.

When the guest requests the return of the property they pass over the receipt and sign the receipt book for the return of the envelope with the seal intact. The cashier verifies the guest's signature against the original and clips the receipt back into the receipt book. The book in this way is evidence of a completed transaction. A quick control check can be made by counting the envelopes in the safe and comparing the number with the number of receipts currently issued. Although this is a secure system, it does mean that a new envelope has to be used for each transaction, even if a guest only wishes to remove part of their property from the deposit. A similar system adopts two-part receipts which are attached to specially printed envelopes stored in the cashier's office (Fig. 2.5).

Safe-deposit boxes

Larger hotels utilise individual deposit boxes for property. The individual boxes are large enough to take personal property such as jewellery, passports, money and traveller's cheques. Larger items such as briefcases, or even fur coats, have to be stored separately. The boxes are stored in individual safes which are

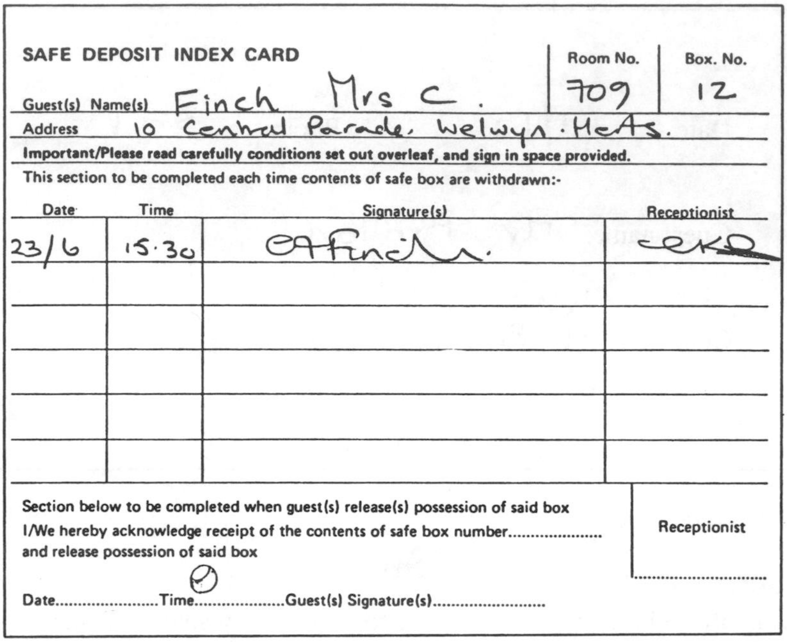

SAFE DEPOSIT INDEX CARD

Room No.	Box. No.
709	12

Guest(s) Name(s) Finch Mrs C.

Address 10 Central Parade, Welwyn. Herts.

Important/Please read carefully conditions set out overleaf, and sign in space provided.

This section to be completed each time contents of safe box are withdrawn:-

Date	Time	Signature(s)	Receptionist
23/6	15.30	C. Finch	

Section below to be completed when guest(s) release(s) possession of said box

I/We hereby acknowledge receipt of the contents of safe box number....................
and release possession of said box

Date......................Time..................Guest(s) Signature(s)........................

Receptionist

Fig. 2.6 *A safe-deposit index card.*

secured by two locks. The first lock is opened by a key that is common to every safe; this key is held by the cashier. The second lock has an individual key, which is issued to the guest who signs the deposit slip (Fig. 2.6). The safe can only be opened when both keys are in the locks. The guest and the cashier must both be present. Each time a guest wishes to remove property, they sign the slip. The cashier countersigns to authorise the guest's signature, and the box is opened with the two keys. These deposit boxes are located in the front office area, where both guests and staff have access to them. Safe-deposit facilities are only offered to people whilst they are residents in the hotel.

Individual room safes

Individual room safes are becoming increasingly popular, since the guest has total control of their valuables, and can access them at any time. The safe is situated in the room, often by the minibar, and is operated by a code number, which the guest programs in on arrival. The safe can be opened and closed any number of times, and the number can be changed at will. Obviously the guest needs to be sure they will remember the number, since there is no other way of opening the safe, but it provides an ideal place to store passports, money and jewellery, and since it is all together it is unlikely that anything will be left behind (Fig. 2.7).

Fig. 2.7 An *individual room safe*.

Cash handling

Every hotel should have some basic rules around the handling of cash. At the very least, they should include the following rules:

• Count all cash in a secure place.
• Limit access to the cashier's office.
• Record the daily float reconciliation.
• Vary the route, time and day of banking.

Guest arrivals and check-out

There is always a potential problem when a guest arrives without a prior reservation. In most hotels it is now standard procedure to request some form of prepayment from chance guests. In many places even guests who have made a booking are asked to give a printout of their credit card, and few people object to this practice. A cash deposit is of limited use, since hotel prices mean that a substantial sum of money would need to be lodged with the cashier if the hotel was to ensure they would not be out of pocket in the case of a walk-out. Essential security measures are not confined to cash handling, and the safeguarding of the hotel's interests. Occasionally the hotel may be the venue for a meeting which is not public knowledge, or a VIP may arrive and not wish to be troubled by the press. These are also security issues, which must be treated sensitively by the reception and other front of house staff if the hotel is to retain a good reputation.

During check-out the cashier needs to be vigilant, since there are many ways of defrauding the hotel, and familiarity with all methods of payment is essential. In most large hotels a security officer will keep front office staff updated with the latest forgeries and warn them of any known criminals in the area. Mistakes do happen, however, and even the most experienced cashiers are sometimes deceived.

Security incidents

There are many types of security hazards in a hotel, ranging from missing items to bomb threats. The nature of a hotel lobby means it is very difficult to keep an eye on people and belongings, especially during the busy periods when guests are checking in and out. Many hotels have set procedures in case of bomb threats, or similar incidents, and staff should familiarise themselves with these on a regular basis. Minor incidents should be reported to the supervisor on duty, while major incidents warrant raising the alarm. If all staff are vigilant, observant and pay attention to detail, the hotel will be a safer place for everyone.

A number of specialist companies offer lighting and video monitoring for vulnerable places such as car parks or other well-known danger spots. Electric security systems can include safety lighting and alarm communications, and can be as obvious or as discreet as the hotel wishes.

Health and safety

Injury time

One employee in the hotel and restaurant sector died and a further 486 received serious injuries in work-related accidents last year, according to figures published by the Health and Safety Commission. The annual report, covering the year from 1 April 95 to 31 March 96, also reveals that 725 members of the public, and nine self-employed workers were seriously hurt.
(*Caterer and Hotelkeeper*, 24 October 1996)

Health and safety is the responsibility of all employees, employers and customers, and all of these groups of people should be encouraged to take an active part in keeping the hotel and its surroundings safe.

The Health and Safety at Work Act was passed with two main aims:

• to protect employers and employees;
• to increase the safety awareness of those at work.

While the law imposes a general duty on the employer to safeguard the health and safety of their employees, it is also fairly specific about the duties and responsibilities of employees. These include the following:

• to take reasonable care of the health and safety of themselves and others in the workplace;
• to co-operate with the employer in meeting or complying with the requirements in relation to health and safety;
• not to interfere with, or misuse anything provided in the interests of health and safety or welfare.

The law is there for the protection of everyone, and it is in everyone's interest to follow it.

In addition to the responsibilities outlined above, many employers will also introduce their own health and safety policies, and appoint a member of staff to act as the health and safety representative for the workforce. While there may be one policy that applies to the entire hotel, there may also be department-specific policies. Many accidents in the hotel and catering industry occur through

- misuse of equipment
- poor lifting
- wet floors
- haste
- distraction

Clearly every department will have its own hazards, and department heads will often be asked to perform a **risk assessment** in order that potential hazards can be identified, and staff warned of them.

Regulations such as COSHH (Control of Substances Hazardous to Health) are in force throughout the entire hotel, but areas such as housekeeping, where cleaning products are stored, are especially vulnerable. The regulations include not only

- labelling instructions
- storage instructions
- usage instructions
- protection requirements

but also requirements that employers are required to inform, instruct and train employees with regard to the risks and precautions associated with the safe handling of these substances.

Fire precautions

Fire is always a terrifying experience, but in a hotel it is particularly so, since guests are in unfamiliar surroundings. It is essential, therefore, that staff are fully experienced in fire drills and practices, and are familiar with all the entrances, exits and assembly points of the hotel.

Fire is caused in a number of ways, often by simple incidents which escalate. Some examples are as follows:

- Human error — e.g. fat fires in the kitchen; careless disposal of cigarettes.
- Electricity — e.g. overloaded plugs; worn wires.
- Maintenance — e.g. old, untested equipment; lack of a planned replacement programme.
- Cleaning substances — e.g. inflammable substances incorrectly stored; careless smoking.

All fires need three elements to sustain them:

- heat
- oxygen
- combustible material

so all fire-fighting equipment is designed to remove at least one of the elements and so starve the fire. All establishments will have their own procedures, both for reporting fires and for evacuating, and staff should ensure they are familiar with them. Hotels in the UK are required to hold a Fire Certificate, which is issued after a fairly rigorous inspection. A 'fire safety checklist' would include many of the following points:

Fire alarm
Call points easily accessible
Easy to operate
Tested regularly

Sprinkler system
Activates automatically
Overhauled and serviced regularly

Fire safety training
For all staff
On a regular basis
Appointment of 'Fire Marshals' from staff

Directional signs
Easy to follow
Well displayed
Illuminated

Emergency lighting
Visible in public areas
Corridors
Escape routes

Fire doors
Kept closed

Fire exits
Clearly indicated
May be numbered
Clear and uncluttered
Easy to open in an emergency

Escape routes
Fire evacuation plan available
Provide alternative escapes from all over building
Free of obstruction and hazard

Fire notices
Brief
Easy to follow
Well distributed

Care of the customer

So far we have looked at several ways in which we care for the physical well-being of the customer. Some of the things we have examined, such as security, also contribute to the mental well-being of our customers. We want them to be happy, relaxed and satisfied.

Why?

'Why' is easy: we want customers to come back. Once they have experienced a product or a service which they have enjoyed, they will want to repeat it. You, in reception, can ensure that their experience starts off satisfactorily.

How can we achieve this?

We can achieve this by displaying good personal skills, good verbal and non-verbal communications, and ensuring that a welcoming smile is always part of the service. Remember that every customer makes a contribution towards your salary, so you have an additional reason for wanting them to come back!

Most customers are not difficult; they are away from home, and want a pleasant stay in comfortable and familiar surroundings. Many customers will even excuse the odd occasion when things go wrong, but inevitably there are those who are rude, and even some who actually enjoy complaining. Some customers may come in and demand the impossible or make a scene – often these people are really very insecure, and they need to assert their authority in this way to make themselves feel important. Prevention is often the best way of dealing with a situation like this, and if you can learn to anticipate problems before they arise you will find this a very effective way of handling awkward clients and situations. This is a skill that can be learnt, so do not despair if it does not work at first.

There are a few general rules for dealing with complaints, and in addition many hotels have standard procedures to follow, to ensure that any real complaints are dealt with and rectified.

Handling complaints

A specialised and important applied social skill is that of dealing with complaints from guests. Normal responses often follow the pattern of 'It's not my fault', 'Oh no I didn't', 'It wasn't me', and other similar phrases. All that these achieve is the provocation of further argument. In dealing with complaints the receptionist should follow the points given below:

- Listen attentively: it is necessary to show that attention is being given.
- Do not interrupt: an interruption will encourage the complainant to carry on louder and longer.
- Wait until the person has completely finished: before saying anything at all, be certain that the guest has completely finished talking, rather than just taking a pause for breath.
- Apologise: a short clear apology should be the first thing the receptionist offers. It should be clear and concise, and should not be qualified in any way by an excuse or explanation.
- Speak normally: a guest complaining is often further aggravated by a receptionist whose voice rises to match that of the irate guest. The result is an unseemly slanging match which may be watched by other guests and staff members.
- Summarise the complaint: repeating the essence of a complaint serves two purposes. Firstly, it ensures that everything has been covered and that there has been no misunderstanding about the cause of the complaint. Secondly, a factual dispassionate summary helps to defuse the situation as it cannot produce further dispute.
- Explain what action will be taken and how quickly. It is important that when giving an explanation of action the guest is not given the impression that 'buck passing' is being carried out. By giving a definite time, the guest is encouraged that something will be done about the grievance.

If a guest is particularly irate, the receptionist should aim to remove the scene to somewhere more private, such as an office, or adjacent lounge. In doing this, the receptionist will remove the physical barrier of the reception desk from the confrontation, for a desk or table can also be a psychological barrier.

Customer loyalty

The best way to ensure that customers return time and time again is by promoting their customer loyalty. Loyal customers are obviously happy customers, and in order to keep them happy we need to know their likes and dislikes. This can be done very easily by recording information each time they stay in the hotel, stored simply on the rear of the registration card (Fig. 2.8, overleaf). New technology has made it much easier to collect guest history, or customer data. It is also possible to target those who stay on a regular basis, so that we can keep them updated of special offers, or mail out any associated services that may be of interest. Many organisations have branded in-house company credit schemes, and these are another reason to keep your customer loyal, and ensure they return.

The most important thing to remember about the customer is not that they are always right, but that they always have a choice.

Date of Arrival	Rm	No. nts	Rate £ . p	Spend £	Call time	Paper	Rest. booking	Notes	Init- ials

Fig. 2.8 *Guest history is an important part of customer loyalty: a guest's details can be stored on the back of the registration card.*

Roles, responsibilities and attributes of a receptionist

The reception staff are the key to the success or failure of customer care.

Why?

Are they more important than the hall porter, or the chef – or even the General Manager? Well, in some ways this is so. The role of the receptionist is so important because it can make or break the stay from the very moment when the enquiry is made for a booking.

How?

A prospective guest contacts the hotel to see if there is any availability on the night they wish to stay. No sales involved here, you may think – the guest is doing all the work. This is so, but imagine the following situation:

CLIENT: Do you have a single room for tomorrow evening?
RECEPTIONIST: No, I'm very sorry, we're busy tomorrow night.

Of course you can't help being busy; after all, that is what the hotel is there for, but the receptionist *could* have said a number of other things, offered some alternatives, asked if the guest could stay any other time, or even offered to recommend somewhere else. The whole point is that the guest *only* talks to the receptionist in a case like that. It doesn't matter if you have the best rooms in town, if the chef is world famous, or if the general manager is the most efficient, because the chances are the guest will never find out.

The role of the receptionist is vital to the efficient running of the hotel.

When questioned, people often say they want to be a receptionist because they like meeting people, but this is only part of the job. A good receptionist has a great many skills, and to be good with people is only one part of the job, or one of the attributes that is needed.

What do they do? What are the main responsibilities?

Reception must be able to **welcome** the guests, and make them feel at home, without being too familiar. They must be able to create a good **first impression**, or the guest may never get further than the reception desk. They must be able to create an impression of **efficiency**. They must be **sensitive** to unusual requests or situations.

The welcome
You may smile and say 'Welcome to the hotel' hundreds of times in your working week, but remember that for each client it is a first. It doesn't matter if they are with you for business or leisure purposes, they are away from home and they have chosen your hotel. Be sure they don't regret it. Smile as if you mean it, and remember to make every welcome a special occasion for each individual who arrives. Also remember the tours and groups. Just because they travel together doesn't mean they are any less important, or less welcome. So remember when you say 'Welcome to the hotel' that we really mean it, because we want everyone to come back.

The first impression
This is another area which is just so important that it cannot be stressed enough. When clients arrive, the impression they get will remain with them throughout their stay. They judge the hotel not only by the way you act, but also by the way you look. Would you be happy to go into a hairdresser where the receptionist looked untidy and not very clean? You might expect the salon to be the same. So it is with the hotel: the guests will judge it by how you look and act.

An efficient manner

However busy the desk is, there is clearly a difference between very busy and highly disorganised. Which would you prefer if you were staying in a hotel? Certainly for many people if they see that the reception staff cannot cope they begin to feel doubtful about things like telephone messages, important faxes which may not find them, and other details which form part of everyday working life. The 'people skills' are important in this job, but so are administrative details. Let your clients know that you are on top of the job, and that you can be trusted to deal with their affairs.

A sensitive approach

There are always a number of situations which demand a caring or sensitive approach. A number of people have disabilities and, while they do not wish to be treated differently from others, they have certain needs which must be identified and dealt with during their stay. Families with very young children will need some special care, or help until they have settled in. Everyone is in reception because they like people, so be sure to make everyone know that you are there to help.

The role of the receptionist

The receptionist is a bit like the hub in the centre of a wheel. All the departments need to lock into the centre piece in order for the system to operate (Fig. 2.9).

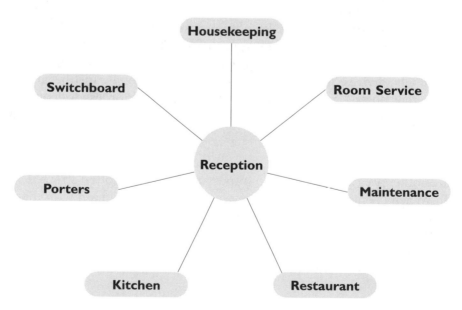

Fig. 2.9   *Reception is like the hub in the centre of the wheel.*

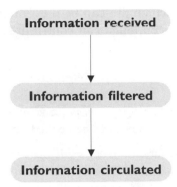

Fig. 2.10 *Information should be sorted and filtered.*

Once one of the spokes is broken, the system will not work effectively. This is why it is essential that all departments **communicate** with each other. The role of the receptionist is centred around the need to communicate.

Virtually all the information that is received in a hotel comes in via reception. What reception must do is act as a filter, and send out the information that is useful to other departments. Not everyone will want the same information; in fact some information is confidential, and should not be circulated widely (Fig. 2.10).

Communication between departments

Communication is a vital part of the role of the reception, and of the smooth running of the hotel. Everyone is aware of the importance of communication between a few key areas:

Kitchen ↔ Restaurant
Reception ↔ Housekeeping

but real communication goes much further than two departments talking to each other, however essential that is. For the hotel to really succeed in providing guests with the service that they require, communication must extend even beyond department level, and good communication skills have never been so easy to achieve as they are today.

Self-assessment questions

1   List five areas which pose potential security risks in a hotel.
2   What are the advantages of electronic keys?
3   Describe an efficient system of safety-deposit facilities in a busy airport hotel.
4   State the main employee obligations under health and safety.

5   State the main ways in which fire can be prevented in hotels.
6   Explain how the hotel receptionist can contribute to customer satisfaction.

Assignment

A serious miscalculation in last night's reservations led to a number of unpleasant incidents when guests had to be booked out at other hotels.

One lady in particular was furious, having made her reservation six months earlier, and written to confirm. She insisted she would never return, and that she would be making a complaint to the head office of the company.

The next day, however, she does return, and if possible she is even more angry. She was expecting a number of telephone calls and faxes, and a caller. None of the phone calls or faxes were re-directed to her new hotel, and when the caller arrived he was directed to another hotel, which was not the one where she was staying. The final insult is when she meets a colleague from her company who is staying in your hotel, despite the fact that he arrived at 2130 hours last night, approximately three hours later than she did.

Tasks

1   Explain how this situation could occur – why *should* she have been booked out when her colleague was given a room?
2   Describe how this situation should be dealt with.
3   List the social skills that would need to be employed when handling this client.
4   What methods could be employed to try and persuade the client back on a return visit?

CHAPTER 3

The Reception Office and Communications

After studying this chapter you should be able to

- list the main types of communication in use
- identify appropriate ways of communicating
- explain why good personal presentation is important
- identify the main office duties in reception
- outline legal responsibilities of the front office
- describe recent advances in telecommunications

Communications

One of the key skills for a hotel receptionist is that of communication. This is not just a simple dialogue between the receptionist and the guest, but a part of the job that underpins all other tasks and duties. In some form or another, this simple skill plays a part in every aspect of the work.

Communication between people can be made in a variety of ways: sometimes nothing is said and yet the meaning is clear. The main methods of communication between individuals are as follows:

- verbal
- non-verbal
- written
- telecommunications

These can be broken down again in a number of different ways; for example, verbal communication can be face to face, or by telephone. Each has its place and its advantages and disadvantages, but a good receptionist will be equally at home with the use of any of them.

Verbal communication

Good verbal communication is essential in most jobs, but rarely does it play such an important part as in the reception office.

Most hotels place a good deal of importance upon the way in which their receptionist speaks, particularly since the receptionist is often the first link with the public. Because of the nature of the work it is important to use a clear and regular tone, varying the pitch so it is not boring, and pronouncing words clearly, including the beginnings and ends of words. Most hotels now deal with national or international clientele, many of whom may have only a limited grasp of the language of the country they are visiting, so strong regional accents can pose a problem.

While it is without doubt essential to speak clearly and without ambiguity to ensure effectiveness, many people omit the most important aspect about communicating – the art of listening. If the reception staff are unable to listen properly, the wrong information could be communicated – often with disastrous results. The reception office of a hotel could be compared to a clearing house in banking. The information arrives, is sorted, and is then redirected to the appropriate place. Often reception staff are dependent on other departments to send them information, but once received it is the responsibility of reception to ensure that all other sections are made aware of any changes or new developments (Fig. 3.1).

If you cannot rely upon your memory, take notes, or identify and highlight the important points. If you are unsure about something, check or question the information that you have received. Above all, listen, and act upon what you have heard. There are some people who ask questions and then do not listen to

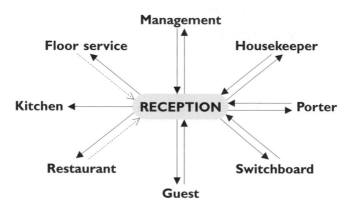

Fig. 3.1 *Reception as the clearing house.*

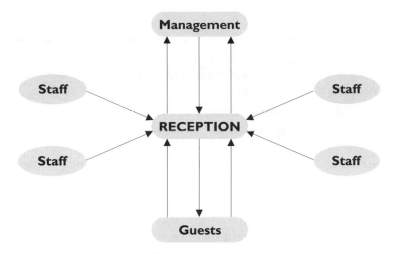

Fig. 3.2 *Reception is the buffer.*

the answer. This is not only pointless but very rude. Be interested and listen to the communication that is directed at you.

The receptionist is expected to be able to deal with many different types of people, some of whom will require special treatment. Those who are deaf or hard of hearing will understand perfectly providing communication is properly carried out. There is no need to shout but use clear speech, pronouncing words clearly, and this should prove effective. It is important to face the client and ensure diction is clear.

It is particularly important in reception to develop the skill of communication at all levels. The reception staff are the buffer between management, guests and other staff, and communication skills will be required when dealing with all groups of people (Fig. 3.2).

The guest

The reception staff must communicate with the guest in such a way that a good first impression is assured, for the first impression is of the utmost importance. Communication with the guest may be both formal and informal. The client will need to give and receive information and the receptionist should ensure that this is done quickly and efficiently.

The client may also, however, be far from home and may occasionally like an informal conversation. It is quite possible to develop your communication skills in this way and create a favourable impression while maintaining and displaying a professional attitude at all times.

Management

Your communication with management or supervisors will usually be of a formal nature. It will frequently involve the giving and receiving of information, and the people to whom you report will want to see effective communication for several reasons:

- the standards of the organisation will be maintained;
- potential problems or complaints will be identified early and eliminated at source;
- poor communications often lead to disillusionment and lack of motivation, which may result in unnecessary staff turnover.

Peers

Communication with your colleagues will be different again, in that while they will be formal in content (e.g. advising the housekeeper of moves, enquiring about baggage from the porters) it will be informal communication in that you are all on a similar level. The way in which you communicate with your peers reflects ultimately upon the smooth running of the hotel. Inevitably there will be occasional clashes of personality but these should never be allowed to evelop to the stage where they are detrimental to the hotel. A negative attitude affects an entire shift, and everyone very quickly becomes unsettled. The hotel business is first and foremost about people, and that means enjoying the company of all types: young, old, either gender and all nationalities. The ability to work as part of a team cannot be overemphasised: an individual who can do the work but is a 'loner' has no future in front office.

Non-verbal communication

This describes all the silent ways in which you display your feelings. Non-verbal communication is conveyed in your facial expression, which can show a welcoming smile or a forbidding frown. Most of us are aware that we have 'good' days and 'bad' days, but in the reception they must all appear, at least, to be good days.

A favourable and welcoming expression can be readily created by observing several elementary non-verbal aspects of behaviour.

Neat appearance

A neat appearance is essential at all times in front office, as an individual neatly presented gives the impression of a well-organised and well-run department (Fig. 3.3). Imagine how quickly you would become disillusioned if you went for

Fig. 3.3 A neat appearance is essential in reception.

an interview for a job and the personnel manager had dirty fingernails or a grease-marked jacket.

Personal hygiene

Personal hygiene is a very basic aspect of non-verbal communication, but one that cannot be overemphasised. Remember that an important front office task is selling accommodation, and reception staff are frequently required to show guests to rooms. The guest will not be impressed if the atmosphere in the lift is unpleasant, and the sale may well be lost. At the very least, a busy receptionist needs a daily bath or shower, a deodorant and carefully selected clothes, which can be washed easily, and will not retain unpleasant perspiration smells.

Posture

Both sitting and standing postures should be carefully attended to. Not only will the correct posture make you less tired at the end of the day but it can reflect efficiency and enthusiasm, or show disenchantment.

The whole attitude of the individual is frequently portrayed by the way in which they stand. Different postures can suggest shyness, reluctance, aggressiveness, willingness, etc. Be sure to display an upright stance with arms unfolded – a confident yet welcoming posture.

Eye contact

Use of correct eye contact is one of the vital skills that is essential to any 'people' industry. It is the non-verbal equivalent of using someone's name. It establishes a personal contact, and warmth and humour are only two of the important emotions that can be expressed through eye contact. It is most disconcerting to have a conversation with someone who refuses to meet your eyes, and many people assume that one who avoids eye contact is untrustworthy. In fact, it more frequently suggests insecurity or shyness, neither of which is an attribute suited to front office work.

'People' skills

What skills are required for carrying out the work of a receptionist and how can they be recognised?

Most hotel staff are recruited after an interview. The picture that an interview gives, however, is often only a partial view of the applicant, for the person applying for the job may try and minimise the traits that they feel would debar them from work as a receptionist.

A list of attributes for the 'perfect' receptionist often sounds similar to the attributes required for perfection in any person (or any other customer-contact job). There is much discussion over whether or not it is possible to train employees to be smart, socially skilled, diplomatic, systematic and so on.

Possibly the most important requirement for the receptionist is an ability (and willingness) to learn. It is unlikely that a recluse will apply to work where they would be in constant contact with people, so, in this respect, applicants will be self-selecting.

A foreign language may be a useful asset in international hotels, but for the bulk of hotels in the UK, a good, clear command of the English language would be adequate. Foreign language needs may be met in smaller hotels by other members of staff, or the provision of phrase books, which invariably deal with the needs of hotel guests

Social skills

Social skills have been described as the way in which a person behaves towards others in different social situations. This can be characterised by the difference between a receptionist's behaviour towards a VIP guest and their behaviour towards the page who has been detailed to accompany the guest to the room. The receptionist will adopt a different style in each case.

Social skills are achieved by the co-ordination of verbal and non-verbal behaviour in a given situation. Equally important is the perception of cues from the other person.

To gain an assessment of a person, it is normal to evaluate information not only from what is said, but the way in which it is said, the bearing or posture, and the gestures the person makes. In addition, important clues are gained from clothing, accessories and luggage. All of this is co-ordinated, often subconsciously, to produce an assessment. For the receptionist, this is very important. Within a few moments, a receptionist may have to decide whether or not to request a deposit. In sales too, the ability to sum up a customer quickly is important. Should the guest be offered a more expensive room? Or should 'value for money' be emphasised?

Airline companies train their staff to quickly recognise passengers who are showing signs of nervousness, and to handle them with extra care to give them reassurance.

Social skills, like any other skill, can be acquired. They deal with feelings and behaviour: it is essential that careful attention is given to any training programme that includes training in social skills. For a receptionist, certain simple social skills are easily acquired.

An attentive manner
In listening to a customer, the receptionist should be interested and concerned about what is being said. It is important not to fiddle with a pencil or to move things around on the desk – these actions suggest boredom.

Eye contact
It is remarkable that some front office staff manage to deal with guests without ever looking them in the eye. The impression once again is of disinterest and shallowness. Eye contact should be established and used throughout any dealings with guests.

Tone of voice
The tone of voice used is as important in conveying meaning as what is actually being said. It is not enough to say, 'I am sorry, sir'; it must be said with the correct inflexion of speech. For most people, a pleasant voice speaks not too loud and not too fast. An alarming trait is that of shouting at foreigners in the hope that they will understand through the sheer volume of noise.

Use of guests' names
At every opportunity the guest's name should be used. This personalises the conversation, and is clear evidence of interest and personal attention. In

addition, it assists reception staff in remembering the names of individual guests. Some hotel companies train their front office staff to address the guest by name at least three times during registration. Conversely, it is extremely rude to refer to customers by their room number, such as, '309 would like to know how much the bill is'. Even in large hotels, it is possible to use guests' names by glancing quickly at the room status system or the key card when being asked for a room key.

Personal presentation

All the above attributes help to contribute to the overall impression of the receptionist and the hotel. Good social skills will not only increase self-confidence and effectiveness, but will also create a favourable impression of the hotel, and inspire customer confidence in the receptionist and the department. A neat and tidy appearance is obviously important in order to convey the vital good first impression. A receptionist should aim to be clean, neatly clothed and well groomed. Many hotels now provide staff with a uniform. This helps to create a professional image, and makes it easier for the guests to recognise staff members. For male staff this is often a business suit, with a pastel shirt and company tie, although many hotels have once again reverted to the traditional pin stripe suits, with white shirt and grey tie. In a very few luxury hotels it is still customary for the male reception and management staff to change into dinner jackets during the evening shift.

Uniform for female staff is more varied, and may be a neat tailored dress, a blouse and skirt or a smart suit. Sometimes different grades of staff are given variations of a basic uniform style, which serves to show their status in the organisation. Whatever the uniform, a receptionist should ensure that it is kept as clean and as well pressed as if it were their own clothing. If the selection of the clothing is left to the receptionist, it is important that it is smart and business-like, yet comfortable. The latest fashions frequently look out of place in the work situation and it is wise to choose something that is traditional and in keeping with the environment. Particular attention should be paid to accessories and jewellery. As a rule, they should be kept to a minimum, especially if a uniform is worn, since they can easily detract from the overall effect of uniformity which should characterise front office staff.

Written communication

Written communication forms a major part of the work of the reception office. It may be handwritten, typewritten or transmitted by fax or computer, but certainly most important information will be written in a permanent way.

Basically the written communication and documentation in front office may be divided into two categories: internal and external.

Internal

Internal communication may often be informal and brief, e.g. the housekeeper notifying reception of ready rooms, or reception notifying other departments of an arrival. Regardless of their apparent informality, this form of communication is vital and must be legible, with accurate and unambiguous information. Communications of this nature must also be distributed with all speed to ensure that each department is in possession of up-to-date information.

Documents in common use for internal communication are many and varied but could include some of the following:

- memos
- arrival and departure lists (Figs 3.4 and 3.5)
- guest lists
- tour rooming lists
- function lists

Other in-house communication systems in common use include the following:

- pocket paging ('bleeps'): an electronic radio device small enough to carry in the pocket, activated by the switchboard operator to call senior staff to the telephone;
- public address system: useful for paging guests and staff, but must be used with discretion;
- internal telephones for use between offices, and occasionally between sister hotels;
- in-house video channel to advertise the hotel's facilities.

External

For many potential guests the written communication that they receive from a hotel may be their first contact with the establishment.

A letter or fax that is badly written or typed, with incorrect spelling, gives a very bad impression and many guests will equate the standard of letter writing with the service provided by the hotel.

If the communication is handwritten, it must be clear and legible. If it is typewritten it must be accurate, without errors and following the correct format. The information that is conveyed should be up-to-date and without ambiguity. Many hotels have adopted a standard or form letter for confirmations (Fig. 3.6, page 50) for the occasions when they still confirm bookings. This eliminates repetitive typing and ensures that all relevant information is included. Many hotels no longer send confirmations, preferring instead to rely upon a release system or communication by computer/fax.

```
┌──────────────────────────────────────────────┐
│  ARRIVALS FOR 21AUG 97      21AUG 97   11:32   │
│                                                │
│                             DEP.DATE STAT      │
│  Amabily R Mr          TDBN 1 25AUG 97 GTD     │
│  Anderton C Ms         OSNN 1 23AUG 97 GTD     │
│  Benton C Ms           OFTN 1 22AUG 97 GTD     │
│  Berg R Mr             OSNN 1 22AUG 97 GTD     │
│  Brand A Mrs           OSNN 1 23AUG 97 GTD     │
│  Burdett Mr            OSNN 1 22AUG 97 GTD     │
│  Carter J Mrs          OSNN 1 22AUG 97 GTD     │
│  Clegg A Mr            OSNN 1 22AUG 97 GTD     │
│  Coucill J Mr          OSNS 1 22AUG 97 GTD     │
│  Dowrick T Mr          OSNN 1 22AUG 97 GTD     │
│  Farrell S Mr          OSNN 1 22AUG 97 GTD     │
│  Green L Ms            OSNN 1 22AUG 97 GTD     │
│  Gregory Mrs           TDBS 1 23AUG 97 GTD     │
│  Han Mr                OSNN 1 25AUG 97 GTD     │
│  Hawthorne P Miss      OFTN 1 22AUG 97 GTD     │
│  Job Q Mr              OFTN 1 22AUG 97 GTD     │
│  Key J Mr              OSNN 1 22AUG 97 PROV    │
│  Lawler J Mr           OSNS 1 22AUG 97 GTD     │
│  Lawson A Mr           OSNN 1 22AUG 97 GTD     │
│  Lawson A Mr           OSNN 1 22AUG 97 GTD     │
│  Lederman D Ms         TDBN 1 22AUG 97 GTD     │
│  Lee Paul Mr           OSNN 1 22AUG 97 GTD     │
│  Mcallister B Ms       OSNN 1 22AUG 97 GTD     │
│  Mcerlean Mr           OSNN 1 22AUG 97 GTD     │
│  Morgan G Mr           OSNN 1 22AUG 97 GTD     │
│  Newsome G Ms          OSNN 1 22AUG 97 GTD     │
│  OBrien C Ms           TDBN 1 24AUG 97 GTD     │
│  Pickford M Mr         OSNN 1 22AUG 97 GTD     │
│  Prentis C Mr          OFTN 1 24AUG 97 GTD     │
│  Price M Ms            OSNN 1 22AUG 97 GTD     │
│  Price S Mr            OSNN 1 22AUG 97 GTD     │
│  Reid B Mr             OSNS 1 22AUG 97 GTD     │
│  Robinson D Miss       TDBN 1 22AUG 97 GTD     │
│  Sallis K Ms           OSNN 1 22AUG 97 GTD     │
│  Seed D Ms             OFTS 1 22AUG 97 GTD     │
│  Smith B Mr            OSNN 1 22AUG 97 GTD     │
│  Teroi Mr              OSNN 1 23AUG 97 GTD     │
│  Walker E Ms           OSNN 1 22AUG 97 GTD     │
│  Williams M Mr         OFTN 1 22AUG 97 GTD     │
│  Wohr Mr               OSNN 1 22AUG 97 GTD     │
│  Wright N Mr           OSNN 1 22AUG 97 GTD     │
│  XushengMo Mr          OSNN 1 22AUG 97 GTD     │
│  Cole A Mr         CAN OSNN 1 22AUG 97 PROV    │
│  Crooks P Mr       CAN OSNN 1 22AUG 97 PROV    │
│  Grace D Mr        CAN OSNN 1 22AUG 97 PROV    │
│  Hipkiss P Ms      CAN OFTN 1 22AUG 97 PROV    │
│  Knight A Ms       CAN OSNN 1 22AUG 97 PROV    │
│  Knoll Tba         CAN OSNN 1 22AUG 97 PROV    │
│  Knoll Tba         CAN OSNN 1 22AUG 97 PROV    │
│  Laud C J Mr       CAN OSNN 1 22AUG 97 PROV    │
│  Meeting Room      CAN MAR  1 22AUG 97 PROV    │
│  Reely I Mr        CAN OSNN 1 22AUG 97 PROV    │
│  Thompson Mr       CAN OFTS 1 22AUG 97 PROV    │
│  Tse C Ms          CAN OSNN 1 21AUG 97 PROV    │
│  Warwicker J Mr    CAN OFTN 1 22AUG 97 PROV    │
└──────────────────────────────────────────────┘
```

Fig. 3.4   *An arrivals list.*

```
            GUESTS DEPARTED TODAY    21AUG 97       11:33
      NAME      ROOM    NIGHTS EARLY    ADULTS CHILDREN
```

NAME	ROOM	NIGHTS EARLY	ADULTS	CHILDREN
Aalberts Mr	317	000	1	0
Arthurs Paul Mr	210	000	1	0
Ashbridge John Mr	108	000	1	0
Barton D Mr	124	000	1	0
Bayne J Mrs	129	000	1	0
Beach R Mr	225	15	1	0
Bond R Mrs	11	000	1	0
Boundy Gerry Mr	112	000	1	0
Bourdillon M Mr	229	000	1	0
Bowles A Mr	119	000	1	0
Brown C Ms	114	000	1	0
Buckholt Mr	327	2	1	0
Buffini T Ms	224	000	1	0
Burton A Mr	227	000	1	0
Clemo B Mr	320	000	1	0
Clemo H Mr	118	000	1	0
Cunningham B Ms	326	000	1	0
Domoney L Miss	316	000	1	0
Dunnms V	116	000	1	0
Eyre M Mr	131	000	1	0
Fletcher T Mr	206	000	1	0
Fradley G Ms	103	000	1	0
Gibson J Mr	104	000	1	0
Heaton S Mr	205	000	1	0
Herbert John Mr	211	1	1	0
Herridge D Ms	201	000	1	0
Ingrouille P Mr	307	000	1	0
Irwin C V Mr	216	000	3	0
Jackson A Ms	115	000	1	0
Kelly M Mr	106	000	1	0
Key J Mr	217	000	2	0
Koroles E Ms	215	000	1	0
Lavender E Mr	212	000	2	0
Macleod D Mr	209	000	1	0
Mcalinden K Miss	221	000	1	0
Mckee C Mrs	223	000	1	0
Meeting Room	MAR	000	5	0
Meeting Room	CL12	2		0
Middleton S Ms	207	000	1	0
Myers Mrs	126	000	1	0
Oslen M Mr	107	000	1	0
Packman J Ms	309	000	1	0
Pendlebury K Mr	329	000	1	0
Pollard Jim Mr	7	000	1	0
Rosbrook V Ms	111	000	1	0
Russell G Ms	301	000	1	0
Shahimi S Ms	1	000	1	0
Sidders Tony Mr	315	000	1	0
Simcox A Mr	8	000	1	0
Smile B Mrs	4	000	1	0
Walker C J Mr	101	000	1	0
Weatherseed A Mr	314	000	1	0
Williams J Mr	318	000	1	0
Winters Ms	319	000	1	0

```
*** END OF REPORT ***
```

Fig. 3.5   *A departure list.*

Mr "name"
Address 1
Address 2
Address 3
Postcode

8th March1997

Dear Mr "name"

I have pleasure in confirming your booking for accommodation at *the* CASTLE HOTEL, Lincoln. The details of your reservation are as follows:

Arrival date:	**4th June 1997**
Departure date:	**6th June 1997**
Number of nights:	**2**
Type of room:	**Ensuite twin**
Rate:	**£65.00 per night, room & breakfast**
Guaranteed by:	**credit card/letter**
	(including VAT @ 17.5%)

There is much to explore in Lincoln - the Castle and Cathedral are Lincoln's two greatest attractions and yet there are many other sights that your visit should include such as the Brayford Pool (the country's largest inland harbour), Steep Hill, the Mint Wall (Britain's tallest non-fortified Roman structure), which can be found immediately behind the hotel, the Usher Art Gallery and an interesting variety of museums. Most of these attractions can be reached on foot within a few minutes from the hotel, which is ideally situated in the historic centre between the Cathedral and Castle. *the* CASTLE HOTEL, has ample parking, so within ten minutes you can enjoy the natural beauty of the Lincolnshire countryside or in half an hour be deep in the beautiful Wolds on the other side of which is miles of unspoilt coastline. Further details of *the* CASTLE HOTEL and Lincoln can be found on our Internet page, address http://www.SmoothHound.co.uk/hotels/castle.html

We look forward to providing you with a convenient location for your visit to historic Lincoln and to the pleasure of meeting you soon.

Yours truly

Malcolm A J Brown MHCIMA FCFA
Director

Fig. 3.6 *A standard or form letter.*

Documents in common use for external communication may include the following:

- letters
- invoices
- standard confirmations
- requests for payment

Telecommunications

Telephone

No reference to communications would be complete without considering the vital role that the telephone plays in any business operation. Effective communication by telephone will not only assist in selling the hotel, but will also promote an image of efficiency.

The rules that apply to good verbal communication are even more applicable to telephone communication since the client has only the telephone conversation on which to judge the standard of the hotel.

Many hotels insist upon their staff answering the telephone in a certain way, e.g. 'Good morning. The Cross Hotel. Marie speaking. How may I help you?' This quickly becomes standard procedure and ensures that the client receives all the information.

As long as the call is answered promptly with an appropriate greeting the client will feel confident that the organisation is efficient. In addition to the correct greeting, all switchboard operators should be familiar with the procedures for overcoming the most common problems that occur:

- unobtainable numbers
- engaged numbers
- disconnected calls
- emergency calls

Most modern telephone systems enable the guest to dial direct both local and long-distance calls. Help is available through the operator should the guest require assistance, and a range of other services will usually be provided by the switchboard operators:

- credit card calls
- directory enquiries
- general enquiries
- collect/reverse charge calls
- early morning calls

Direct dialling

In most hotels, when direct dialling from guest's rooms was introduced, individual meters for each extension were installed in reception. This enabled the staff to calculate the number of units consumed, cost them according to the charge made by the hotel, and subsequently post the price to the guest's account. Unfortunately this system is not without problems since staff occasionally forget to read the meter, and so the units of one client may be added to the bill of an incoming client. Should a client dispute a charge, it is impossible to check the cost of the call, and much revenue can be lost in this way.

Computerised phone billing

A computerised switchboard enables the billing of telephone calls to be controlled in a much more effective manner Each call is logged with the date and the exact time, the number that was called, how long the call was connected for, the number of units consumed and the cost of the call according to the hotel's charges. This can then be automatically charged to the guest's account, or printed out for the guest to see in case of query, or used for control purposes. The system can also 'bar' extensions, which enables the hotel to control the use of the telephones: various offices may have access to local calls, but not national or international calls, while other offices may not be able to call out at all. If a guest has not acknowledged a request for payment of account, the extension can be barred.

Many hotels have taken advantage of the new technology now available to provide their guests with additional services. These are particularly valuable for the business community, and may well present a good selling point.

Telephone systems can now provide a range of services for both the hotel and the client. The systems are automated, and generally activated through a system known as **voice processing**, which is a combination of computer technology and the spoken word. The systems include a variety of services:

- wake-up calls
- message-waiting facility
- access to hotel services
- voice mail

Wake-up calls

The guest can program their own wake-up call, and they will be called automatically, in a language of their own choice. The system can be set so that the call will be repeated a number of times, after which time the operator will be alerted so that an investigation can be made into the guest's safety.

Message-waiting facility

Here the telephone in the room will display a light to show that a message is waiting for the guest to collect. In addition, the system will 'ring' the guest quietly at intervals until such time as the message is collected.

Access to hotel services

The telephone system can be used to access directly all the hotel services, and to display an up-to-date copy of the guest's bill. Although the guest is virtually self-sufficient, they may decide they do not wish to be disturbed; in that case all their calls can be diverted to the hotel operator, but the individual service is still there if the customer requires it.

Voice mail

When guests arrive, they are allocated an electronic mailbox, and given an individual 'PIN' number. This allows them to empty their mailbox. The hotel may also take advantage of the service by placing a welcome message in the guest's own language, and in some cases they will also provide the guest with the facility to pick up messages for a while after they have left.

Telecommunication systems mean that many of the devices of the past have become virtually obsolete. The telex was very popular, since it enabled bookings to be received when there was no one in advance reservations, and the problem of differing time zones was easily overcome. Very few hotels now use this system, since other methods of communication are faster and easier.

E-mail

This system can be in use both internally and externally, providing that the organisation is networked. It is a way of using the network to both send and receive messages, either from one office to another, or from one organisation to another. Even if the recipient is overseas, the message can be composed and transmitted in a matter of seconds. Attachments can also be sent, so that consultative documents do not need to be reproduced. Use of e-mail within an organisation can significantly reduce the amount of paper generated, since the message need not be printed out, but can be stored in the memory for future reference. The same message may also be sent to any number of people without the need to photocopy or circulate the information. Once a message has been received, the reply can be attached to it, or it can be forwarded to a third party (Fig. 3.7, page 54).

Fax

Fax (or facsimile printing) is simply a way of transmitting a document in its original form from one place to another. Inaccuracies due to transcription errors are thus eliminated, and diagrams and illustrations can be reproduced and received in their exact format. The two machines are linked together by a telephone line and the best description is one of two photocopiers joined by telephone. Most fax machines are of the desk-top variety and consequently small enough to install almost anywhere.

Documents, deeds and other information can be sent automatically 24 hours a day, and messages can be timed to the exact second. Many models feature a delayed transmission with automatic dialling and re-dialling if necessary. This has the dual advantage of overcoming different time zones and also means that messages can be scheduled to be sent when call rates are at their very lowest.

```
From:          "RUSSELL JOSEPH" <POST/JOSEPR>
To:            BAIRDC
Date sent:     Tue, 26 Aug 1997 10:16:46 +00
Subject:       Meeting at Woods Hotel


Would it be possible to meet in the hotel lobby on Tuesday 26 August
1997 at 11am? If you are agreeable to this we can have lunch after
the meeting in the coffee shop which now has an extensive menu.

Regards

Russell Joseph




Chris Killingworth-Baird        -- 1 --        Tue, 26 Aug 1997 10:19:40
```

Fig. 3.7 *A printout of an e-mail message.*

Most machines transmit and receive up to A4 size, although some will accept larger documents.

These machines are rapidly becoming invaluable, not only to the hotel, but also to the many business people staying in the hotel who will gladly pay to use the facility. Many private individuals have fax machines at home, and hotels are rapidly finding that this is service which they must offer (Fig. 3.8). Confirmation by fax is rapidly becoming the norm, and most hotels have a fax cover sheet designed in a similar way to a standard or form letter (Fig. 3.9, page 56).

Increasingly, hotels are using interactive TV sets functioning as room terminals and providing clients with a fax and computer modem as part of the service. Access to the Internet and the WWW is becoming more common. Through the use of closed circuit television, users can follow proceedings elsewhere, and world-wide video conferencing is an important part of many international organisations.

Hotels are faced with difficult and costly decisions if they wish to stay abreast of the rapidly advancing technology which is affecting the business world.

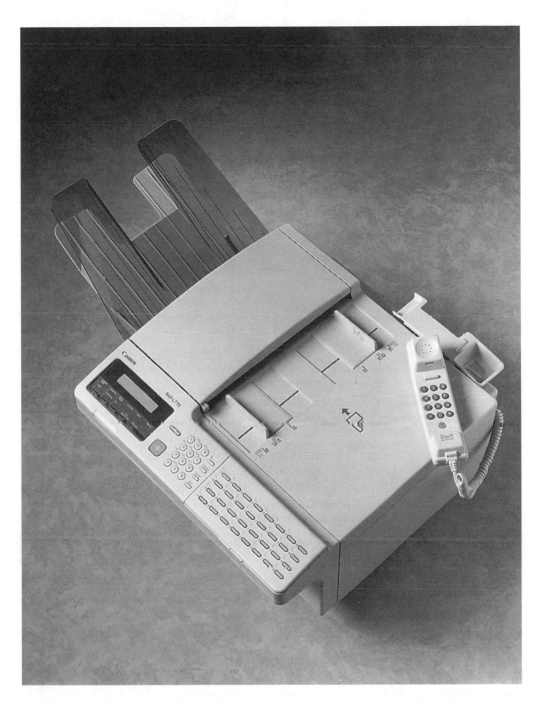

Fig. 3.8 *A fax machine.*

the CASTLE HOTEL

Westgate, Lincoln LN1 3AS
Tel: (01522) 538801 *Fax:* (01522) 575457

FACSIMILE MESSAGE

To:	"Company name"	**Date:**	
Attn:	"Name of contact"	**Our fax number:**	(0)1522 575457
From:	"Your name"	**Your fax number:**	"Their fax number"
Re:	<u>Hotel reservation</u>	**Page no 1 of 1 pages**	

I have pleasure in confirming your booking for accommodation at *the* CASTLE HOTEL, Lincoln. The details of your reservation are as follows:

Arrival date:	**4th June 1997**
Departure date:	**6th June 1997**
Number of nights:	**2**
Type of room:	**Ensuite twin**
Rate:	**£65.00 per night, room, & breakfast**
Guaranteed by:	**credit card/letter**
	(including VAT @ 17.5%)

Further details of *the* CASTLE HOTEL and Lincoln can be found on our Internet page, address http://www.SmoothHound.co.uk/hotels/castle.html

Following are directions to the hotel by car. We look forward to providing you with a convenient location for this visit to historic Lincoln.

Directions.

Head to the North of Lincoln. At the *A15/A46 roundabout* take the exit to *'Historic Lincoln'*. Take the *third exit at the second roundabout* and the *first exit at the third*. Follow the road round as Burton Road turns to the left to become *Westgate*. *the* CASTLE HOTEL is *on your left* at the 'No Through Road'.

Directors:
Malcolm Brown MHCIMA FCFA & Sherry Brown

Fig. 3.9 *A standard fax cover sheet.*

General office practice

The tasks performed in the reception office are in many ways little different from those in any other office. The skills most frequently required will include the following:

- typing/word processing
- filing
- duplicating

Typing/word processing

Much of the typewritten communication will be internal, but letters that are being sent to a prospective client will only result in a sale if they are arranged in a professional manner with the correct form of address. Accurate typing is no longer as important, since a word processor allows for easy correction, but the letter should still be laid out in a formal and recognised fashion, without any spelling errors.

Filing

The main methods of filing in the reception are usually either

- alphabetical   or   • numerical

Guests' accounts are usually filed in room number order (numerical), while registration cards may be filed alphabetically under the name of the client, or numerically under the room number of the guest for the period when they are in the hotel.

Other methods of filing in common use include

- chronological   or   • by subject

Confirmation letters are filed under the date of arrival (chronological) and then under the name of the guest (alphabetical).

Some function and conference business may be filed by subject (e.g. W – Weddings), while others may be filed under the company making the reservation.

Duplicating

The staff in most reception offices will need to circulate information to other departments. If there are no more than a few copies required (e.g. a memo), a photocopy is often sufficient or the required number can be printed off on the computer. On the occasions when a large number of copies are required they may be very occasionally still made by spirit or ink duplicator, or more likely be sent out to be done professionally by a printer.

Additional tasks

Postal services

Particularly in a small hotel where there is no separate enquiry office, the reception staff will need to be conversant with the various postal services available to the hotel. The services most likely to be utilised by both the hotel and guest include the following:

- special delivery
- recorded delivery
- registered post
- business reply service

The receptionist should also be familiar with the various communication services such as Red Star/Parcelforce and private courier services.

The hotel mail will frequently be the responsibility of the reception staff and this includes both incoming and outgoing mail for the hotel, the guests and other staff. Outgoing mail is frequently stamped through a franking machine since this reduces potential pilfering of postage stamps, enables the hotel to keep a check on outgoing mail, and also allows for an advertising slogan to be printed.

Reference sources

Even when there is a separate enquiry office, many guests will still go to reception for advice. The reception office should be well stocked with reference books to enable guests' enquiries to be dealt with efficiently. The material that should be available would normally include the following:

- local maps and guides
- timetables
- information relating to local/national events
- airline information

Many hotels will provide the guests with a system such as teletext, which will allow clients to access information for themselves.

Legal requirements

The receptionist and the law

This section will cover the main points of the law with which a receptionist should be directly involved. With the exception of the manager, a receptionist is the member of staff who is most likely to need knowledge of the law relating to the operation of a hotel and the handling of guests.

Hotels in law

The first problem is, what is a hotel? The Hotel Proprietors Act 1956 lays down responsibility for 'inns'. Most hotels offering accommodation, even the most luxurious establishment in London's Park Lane, will be classed as inns. The name of the establishment cannot be taken as a guide; some establishments entitled 'Private Hotel' may in reality be inns. Likewise, even though an establishment is called an inn, it may not fall within the realm of the Act, for there may be no accommodation to let.

Generally, private hotels are those establishments that choose their guests in some way or another, perhaps by offering accommodation to clergymen only. Finally, the display of the sign limiting liability for loss to guests' property does not indicate that the property is an inn because the notice itself contains a disclaimer (Fig. 3.10, overleaf).

Booking

Bookings and reservations are covered by the law of contract.

The first stage is the offer. A potential guest enquires whether or not accommodation is available on a given night. The receptionist states that there is a room available at £120, for example. The offer has been made.

Next is the acceptance: the guest can either accept the offer, reject it, or make a counter offer. If they accept then the contract is formed. There is no need for written confirmation in law. Naturally, a verbal contract will be more difficult to prove, but it is a contract nonetheless.

Cancellation of bookings is in favour of the guest. If they wish to cancel a booking, the cancellation takes effect the moment they post the letter of cancellation. Should the hotel wish to withdraw, its letter of cancellation does not take effect until it is received by the guest.

Certain groups of people have only limited rights to make contracts. The ones most relevant to hotels are

- persons under the age of eighteen
- the mentally sick
- drunkards
- companies

Registration

Guests at a hotel must provide their full name and nationality. They are not obliged to provide the information themselves (it could, for example, be given by a tour leader or chauffeur), nor are they legally obliged to sign a register. Aliens (overseas visitors) have to provide, in addition, details of their passport number and its place of issue, their next destination and their address there if known.

4 & 5 ELIZ. 2   *Hotel Proprietors Act*, 1956   **CH. 62**

SCHEDULE   <small>Section 2.</small>

NOTICE

LOSS OF OR DAMAGE TO GUESTS' PROPERTY

Under the Hotel Proprietors Act, 1956, an hotel proprietor may in certain circumstances be liable to make good any loss of or damage to a guest's property even though it was not due to any fault of the proprietor or staff of the hotel.

This liability however—

(*a*) extends only to the property of guests who have engaged sleeping accommodation at the hotel;

(*b*) is limited to £50 for any one article and a total of £100 in the case of any one guest, except in the case of property which has been deposited, or offered for deposit, for safe custody;

(*c*) does not cover motor-cars or other vehicles of any kind or any property left in them, or horses or other live animals.

This notice does not constitute an admission either that the Act applies to this hotel or that liability thereunder attaches to the proprietor of this hotel in any particular case.

PRINTED IN ENGLAND BY J A DOLE
Controller and Chief Executive of Her Majesty's Stationery Office and
Queen's Printer of Acts of Parliament.
Reprinted in the Standard Parliamentary Page Size.
1st Impression August 1956
9th Impression July 1984

Fig. 3.10   *The schedule to the Hotel Proprietors Act.*

All this information has to be kept for 12 months. In law there is no requirement for a guest to provide an address, nor even their real name. Naturally, a hotel would be very cautious of a guest who was unwilling to provide their address, or a guest who they thought was using a false name, although this may be common practice among celebrities.

Every guest must register, so it is insufficient for Mr and Mrs Smith to check into a hotel. The full name of Mrs Smith has to be provided, as well as the full name of Mr Smith. The record of guests must be produced to a police officer

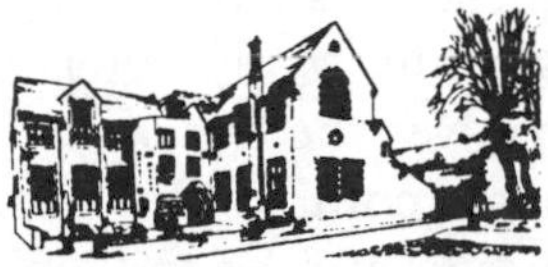

the CASTLE HOTEL
LINCOLN

Directors: *Malcolm Brown MHCIMA FCFA*
Sherry Brown

Registration form

under the Immigration (Hotel records) Order 1972

To be completed by each guest aged Sixteen years or over

Family name: ______________________ Mr/Mrs/Ms/Miss

Forenames: ______________________

Family name (partner): ______________________ Mr/Mrs/Ms/Miss

Forenames: ______________________

Nationality: ______________________

Address: ______________________

____

______________________ Post code: __________

Signature: ______________________ Car reg: __________

Other than British subjects

Passport number:

____

Where issued:

____

Proposed next destination:

____

FOR OFFICE USE

Chance | Advance

Fig. 3.11 *A registration form designed to collect information required by law.*

on request, but if required for any other purpose, need only be provided after a court order (Fig. 3.11).

All this is outlined in the Immigration (Hotel Records) Order 1972 and applies both to inns and private hotels. The exceptions to this are diplomats, their families and staff, who are exempted by the Diplomatic Privileges Act 1964.

Hotels have to accept every traveller who arrives, unless there is a special case for refusal. This may be if the person is in an unfit state to be received, or if the hotel is full. The category 'unfit to be received' would include guests who were drunk. Colour or nationality are not sufficient reasons of refusal to receive guests; this area is covered by the Race Relations Act 1976. A guest who arrived with a known prostitute could also be refused, for it would open the hotel to prosecution as an immoral house.

To avoid argument over such points as whether a person is drunk, or if they are suspected of being a prostitute, the safest course for receptionists to follow is to refuse a guest because the hotel is full. There can then be no question of doubt about the guest's fitness to be received.

The hotel is entitled in common law to request that the guest pays a reasonable amount in advance; there is no obligation to allow guests credit. Many hotels request a deposit greater than one night's room charge to cover the use of extras such as telephones, or the restaurant. It is increasingly common for hotels to request a run of a client's credit card, which will be returned to them on check out in exchange for a completed total of their bill.

Price display

The Tourism (Sleeping Accommodation Price List Display) Order 1977, which came into operation in 1978, requires all hotels and guest houses to display their tariff at the reception desk. This order ensures that the rate for each type of room is clearly shown and the amounts of any taxes and service charges are also displayed. If meals are included, this also has to be made clear.

Service charges must not be stated as a percentage of the rate, but should included in the price charged, so a typical notice should read as follows:

Single room:	£80 per night including VAT and service charge.
Double room:	£106 per night including VAT and service charge.
Suite:	£180–260 per night including VAT and service charge.

Innkeeper's liability

The hotel is liable for loss of guests' property while they are staying at the hotel (strictly, from midnight on the day of arrival to midnight on the day of departure), but is not liable for guests' cars or their contents.

This liability does not extend to cases where loss or damage is caused by an act of God, action by the Queen's enemies, or negligence by the guest or their servants or companions.

If the loss is caused by negligence or action of the hotelier or the staff then the hotel is fully liable, even if it has limited its liability through displaying the statutory notices from the Proprietors Act 1956. This notice limits the liability of the hotel to £50 for any one article, or a total of £100 per guest. It is printed in full in Fig. 3.10 (on page 60).

Section (b) is important for it shows that liability can be full if the property was put into safe deposit or offered for safe deposit.

If a guest were to offer property for deposit, but the receptionist refused it as all the deposit boxes were full, and it was subsequently stolen, then the hotel would be fully liable for the subsequent loss.

The goods do not have to belong to the guests for them to be able to claim. A salesperson could claim for lost samples, for example.

Payment of bill

A hotel may request full payment of the bill in legal tender. In practice this means cash. An offer to pay by any other means need only be accepted at the discretion of the hotel. The Theft Act 1968 has made it easier for guests who leave without paying to be prosecuted. Section 16 allows prosecution of any person who obtains a pecuniary advantage by deception. A guest who gives a cheque in payment, knowing that it will not be met, can be prosecuted. If it is given in good faith, however, this may not be the case.

Innkeeper's lien

Should a guest be unable or unwilling to pay the bill, the hotel may hold the guest's property against payment. Excluded from this are cars and clothing worn by the guest. This does not mean that a guest may be physically restrained from leaving the hotel, for the restraint may constitute an assault.

All the guest's property may be held, even if it is clear that it will more than cover the amount of the bill. There is no need to bargain over the amount that should be left.

The Innkeepers Act 1878 allows the hotelier to auction the goods after six weeks. The auction must be advertised at least one month previously. Any surplus that remains from the sale after deducting the amount of the bill and expenses should be returned to the guest.

Value added tax

VAT is a government tax which is levied on most goods and services, with the exclusion of things such as newspapers and VPOs. Any service charge which is added to the total bill will also be subjected to VAT.

Accurate records of all VAT collected must be maintained, and since prices are frequently shown inclusive of VAT the reception staff must learn to become adept at extracting VAT from the price quoted (Fig. 3.12, overleaf). Officers from HM Customs and Excise are free to inspect the hotel VAT records at any time. Although VAT is a UK tax, most countries have something similar, although the exact figures will differ from one country to another.

the CASTLE HOTEL

Westgate, Lincoln LN1 3AS
Tel: (01522) 538801   *Fax:* (01522) 575457

To: Attn:
         Address 1
         Address 2
         Address 3
         Address 4
         Postcode

VAT number
613 9572 31

VAT invoice for bill numbers:	????
Reference:	????
Tax date:	????

ITEM	VAT Rate	Inclusive of V A T	VAT content	Exclusive of V A T
Accommodation	17.5 %	0.00	0.00	0.00
Breakfast	17.5 %	0.00	0.00	0.00
Luncheon	17.5 %	0.00	0.00	0.00
Dinner	17.5 %	0.00	0.00	0.00
Snacks:	17.5 %	0.00	0.00	0.00
Wine:	17.5 %	0.00	0.00	0.00
Bar:	17.5 %	0.00	0.00	0.00
Newspapers:	0.0 %	0.00	0.00	0.00
Telephones:	17.5%	0.00	0.00	0.00
Sundries:	17.5 %	0.00	0.00	0.00
Sundries:	17.5 %	0.00	0.00	0.00
TOTAL DUE ON THIS INVOICE		**0.00**	0.00	0.00

TERMS OF SETTLEMENT
   Strictly within 28 days of submission of this invoice unless otherwise agreed in writing
   NB   *Late payment will result in withdrawal of corporate benefits.*
        It is our policy to recoupe all costs involved in chasing outstanding payments
CHEQUES
        Cheques to be made payable to 'the Castle Hotel', and sent to the above address

AA   *Directors:*   *RAC*
                          Malcolm Brown MHCIMA FCFA & Sherry Brown

Fig. 3.12 *A standard VAT invoice ready for completion.*

Self-assessment questions

1 List the main methods of non-verbal communication.
2 Give the main types of verbal communication in use in front office.
3 Describe some uses of telecommunications in front office.
4 List the main office skills required by the receptionist.
5 What are the main attributes of a hotel receptionist?
6 Outline the main points of law concerning the registration of guests.

Assignment

A client staying at the hotel has asked to deposit some jewellery which she will not need until the weekend. The receptionist on duty takes the necklace and ear-rings, wrapped in tissue, and puts them in a brown envelope which is sealed in front of the guest. The receptionist marks the envelope 'One diamond necklace and ear-rings' and enters the name of the client and the room number, both on the envelope and in the book kept for that purpose. Unfortunately when the guest comes to collect the envelope it is no longer in the safe.

Tasks

Assuming that the establishment is legally classified as an Inn:

1 Explain the legal implications of this situation.
2 State the financial liability of the hotel.
3 Give ways in which the liability could have been minimised.
4 Referring to Chapter 2, describe an alternative system that would provide the hotel with greater security.

CHAPTER 4

Reservations

After studying this chapter you should be able to

- show how potential bookings are communicated to a hotel
- explain how bookings are recorded, amended and cancelled
- understand how a hotel may control the flow of bookings to maximise revenue

Methods of reservation

All hotels accept reservations or advance bookings for their rooms, in order to achieve high occupancy, and maximise their revenue. The proportion of bookings that are made in advance will vary from 100% in a resort hotel to perhaps 10% in a 'transient' or motorway hotel. Also, the length of time in advance that the guest books (the 'lead' time) will vary from a few hours to many months.

The reception staff need a system that will enable them to

1   check whether a reservation request is possible;
2   record the booking;
3   retrieve the booking at the appropriate time.

It does not matter how the request for a reservation is made; the system of processing it will remain the same. All possible forms a reservation request can take are shown in Fig. 4.1 (overleaf). The immediate request is 'a room for tonight', but the future request could be for 'next week', 'next month' or even 'next year'.

Later in this chapter we will look at methods of choosing between one reservation and another. This is called **yield management**.

Fig. 4.1 *Processing a reservation request.*

Telephone

Telephone bookings are the most common form of booking in many hotels. It is quick, easily accessible and, most importantly, it is interactive – the potential guest can find out immediately if a room is available, if the price is satisfactory, and so on. It also gives the receptionist the opportunity to clarify any necessary points – who will be paying the bill, will the arrival be before 6 p.m., is a restaurant booking wanted, and so on.

Normally, telephone reservations are requested to confirm the booking.

Information required for a reservation

Hotels will vary in the detail and amount of information they require when accepting a booking. Some take a minimum, others will gather a lot, and some will wait until the guest arrives before finding out some of the details.

The minimum can be represented as:
    When?
    How long?

Who?
What type of room?

The hotel will respond with:

Price
Conditions

Before looking at the other information that can be gathered, it will be interesting to examine the basics in more detail.

When?

This is the date. The reservations department needs to clarify the exact date. For example, what is meant by '8/5'? A European would say it is 8th May; but an American would say it is 5th August. Americans often put the month first, particularly when printing dates.

By repeating back the date to a guest, misunderstandings can be avoided. Of course, those misunderstandings could lead to a dishonoured reservation, or a no-show.

Travel and the time

Look how time changes can confuse the picture:

- If you leave US to London at 4 p.m. on the 10th you arrive 6 hours later at 6 a.m. on the 11th.
- Phone New Zealand at 8 p.m. on the 23rd and you will be answered by someone at 9 a.m. on the 24th. It is already tomorrow.

How long?

Here the question is the length of stay; three nights, for example. Again there is a risk of language causing confusion. Some may request arriving 3rd, staying through the 6th. Are they staying for three nights or four?

Who?

An obvious question. B. Patel – but is it Mr, Mrs, Ms or Professor? Also to be clarified is which Patel – has he or she stayed before?

What type of room?

Room types and names vary endlessly. The most common difficulty is understanding the difference between a double (one large bed) and a twin (two beds). Some modern hotels will have two double beds in a room to accommodate families.

Room for confusion

Do you know what each of these is?

SINGLE	QUEEN
STUDIO	KING
SUITE	DOUBLE
JUNIOR SUITE	ROLLAWAY

Price

Yield management has made this question more difficult. Some hotels have now moved away from publishing a tariff. They quote each booking individually depending upon demand. Center Parcs, a well-known holiday company, adopts this method. The price depends upon **when** you want to stay, **how long** you wish to stay for, and **how busy** they expect to be. The majority of hotels, however, still stick to a published tariff.

How much is that room?

A typical enquiry, well handled, may go as follows:

CALLER: Could you tell me how much a room is?

RESERVATIONS: Is that for single or double occupancy?

CALLER: Single.

RESERVATIONS: And when for?

CALLER: Tonight.

RESERVATIONS: A room tonight with private facilities, parking and VAT is £75. Breakfast is charged extra if you take it.

The example in 'How much is that room' shows that it is necessary to clarify the caller's requirements before it is possible to answer the initial question. A single room for a Sunday night in two months' time could easily be a different price. For this reason hotels often develop a standard response to deal with enquiries. They can then be certain that the potential guest knows exactly what is included. Top London hotels often quote room rate *excluding* VAT. This alone could add £31.50 to a £180 room. In the US, rooms are always quoted excluding State Sales Tax which will vary between 3 and 12%.

Further information

The amount of extra information taken by reservations will vary from company to company and location to location. City centre hotels may ask if reserved garage space is required and resort hotels might ask for an estimated arrival time. Listed below are the various questions that may be asked:

- company
- phone number
- fax number
- address
- postcode

- arrival time
- stayed before?
- credit card number
- car reg number
- flight details

- nationality
- smoker/non-smoker
- frequency club number

These details will speed check-in on arrival and identify previous guests.

Postcode generator

In the UK, and in the US with Zip codes, some computer systems will now search and print the address simply from the postcode details. This can cut down keyboard work by 85% and dramatically improve accuracy of address and spelling.

The operator is simply required to type in the house number and name of the guest. Where the majority of customers come from within the host country (UK customers in a UK hotel, etc.), this speeds up the booking process and adds an air of professionalism. There is the element of fraud reduction, as people using false addresses may easily be identified and other security checks can be made.

Fax

The fax combines the speed of the telephone with the permanence of a letter. Most hotels now have a fax machine in the reservations department. There is less opportunity for misunderstanding a reservation request, a confirmation of booking is instantaneous, and it is still interactive – the reservation clerk can converse with the customer. Another important advantage of the fax in reservations departments is that a message can still be sent even though there is no-one on duty at the other end. This is particularly important for hotels with an international clientele. A guest may book from Australia or America without having to check time zones to ensure that someone will be available to take the reservation. Equally, the hotel can fax back a confirmation at any time it wishes.

Letter

Resort hotels have much of their accommodation reserved by letter. Here the guest writes to the hotel with their requirements and length of stay. The lead time is longer, so speed of communication is not so important. A letter of reservation is also useful, for the customer can tell the hotelier about any special requests, and it is clearly more enforceable as a contract in the event of a subsequent non-arrival.

If the guest wishes to charge the account to their company then this can be mentioned in the letter, and the hotel has authorisation which it can verify if necessary.

Computer terminal

This has been the fastest-growing method of booking in recent years. Three routes are possible:

• dedicated company system
• hybrid company/trade system
• Internet access

Dedicated company system

All large chains operate their own reservations system on computer. These are often linked to a 'call centre' which handles central reservations for all properties, either in one country or throughout the world. A typical example is Holidex, operated by Holiday Inns, which handles bookings for over 2000 hotels in over 50 countries around the world. All of the various hotels are linked with each other and the central hub computer by satellite.

Hybrid company/trade systems

These are generally referred to as GDS systems. This stands for Global Distribution Systems. The major systems are operated by consortia of airlines. These have names such as Sabre, Apollo and Amadeus. They book not only hotels, but also airline seats and car rentals. These system terminals are installed in all travel agent offices throughout the world. Further information about GDS is in Chapter 10.

Internet access

Increasingly hotels are taking space on Internet sites and offering guests the opportunity to book via this electronic method. Again, this is covered in Chapter 10.

Personal

Here there is a direct face-to-face contact between the customer and the receptionist. Return bookings are frequently made in this way as guests depart at the end of their stay. The receptionist has the opportunity to find out the maximum information (about late arrival or room type required) and can answer any queries the guest may raise. At quiet times the receptionist may also be able to show the guest the room type and utilise some sales techniques to increase the expenditure of the potential customer.

Recording bookings

The bulk of hotels now record bookings via a computer terminal. This allows amendments and cancellations to be made easily. Further, marketing and sales information can be easily collected and used. Some small hotels may still use a booking diary and booking chart to record reservations. The computer systems simply automate these processes.

Hotel diary

All reservations are entered in the hotel diary under the arrival date. The diary is normally a large, loose-leaf ledger which is constantly updated by the addition of new pages at the back, and the pages for each day's arrivals are removed from the front.

A fresh page is used for each day and if it becomes full, a follow-on page can easily be inserted. The reservation form in Fig. 4.2 has a box for the clerk to tick when the booking has been transferred to the diary. Letter and fax reservations are normally entered straight into the diary.

ROOM RESERVATION

NAME SPARROW G. Mr — ARRIVAL 23/6
NAME — DEPARTURE 24/6
NAME — Refile — Arrival
Departure

SINGLE ☑ RATE £40 — ARRIVAL TIME 23.00
TWIN ☐ RATE
DOUBLE ☐ RATE — GUARANTEED (YES) NO
EXEC. ☐ RATE
SUITE ☐ — PAST GUEST ☑
TYPE RATE
TYPE RATE — Mkt Seg

RESERVATION REQUESTED BY Jan — PHONE 01 246 2648 x 123
COMPANY Birds Ltd — TOWN London
ADDRESS 10 Wellend Walk

REMARKS GTD Late Arr. 2140 - Heathrow

BILL TO Birds Ltd — ACCOUNT NO:

PHONE ☑ VERBALLY ☐ DATE 1/6 — RESERVATION TAKEN BY CKB
TO BE CONFIRMED — BY TELEX ☑ BY LETTER ☐ NOT ☐ — COMPUTER REF:

Fig. 4.2 *Room reservation form.*

NAME	TYPE OF ROOM	NO. OF NIGHTS	RATE	DATE	CONFIRM-ATION	ROOM NO.	REMARKS
WED. 10th June							
Finch Mr. C } Hawks Mr. M }	TB	3	£45	19/2	T/y		Quiet.
Jay Mrs.P.	Suite	4	£80	11/3	C/F		V.I.P.
Sparrow Mr.G.	SB	1	£30	19/4	C/F.		A/c to Birds
Robin Miss R.	SB	2	£30	16/5			See also 24/5+'9/
Starling Mr.H	TB	3	£45	16/5			Canc. T 18/5
Nightingale Tours.	15TB 3DB	4	-	20/3			ARR. 18.00. Buffet 19.30.

Fig. 4.3   *Extract from a hotel diary.*

It can be seen from Fig. 4.3 that reservations are entered chronologically, so finding a particular name on a given day's arrival sheet may take some moments. The remarks column allows the reservation clerk to note any special requirements, such as the account to company of 'Mr Sparrow', and also any subsequent cancellations, and the date of cancellation. This is shown for 'Mr Starling'. Tour or group bookings are normally entered in the diary in the same way as a normal booking, although they obviously represent a larger number of arrivals. If a booking is for two or more people with different names, both names are always noted, so that if mail or messages arrive for the guest, the receptionist is aware of the arrival date.

Multiple dates

'Miss Robin' has reserved accommodation on two other dates in addition to 10th June. All of these are noted in the diary under each arrival date with cross-references to all the others. In this way the receptionist has the maximum information available. The letter booking the accommodation can either be moved forward to the next date after each arrival or, if possible, photocopied, and a copy should be placed under each arrival date.

Reservation procedure

A diary is the most basic form of reservation system. It records the bookings as they come in.

Traditional method

Task

Check chart
Enter on reservation form
Enter in diary
Update chart
Send confirmation
File

Computer method

Task	Equipment
Check chart	VDU
→ Enter booking	Keyboard
→ Update chart	Memory
→ Send confirmation	Word processor
→ Store	Memory

(Simultaneous)

If a booking is cancelled then a simple command to the computer will reverse the process. Depending upon how the program is written, the screen may still display the booking but distinguish it as cancelled. This facility to continue to display a booking may be very useful for amended arrival dates. As all the processes are completed simultaneously, the accuracy and speed of charts, reservation letters and amendments are improved dramatically.

Overbooking too can become more technical, as the computer may be programmed to record the relationship between reservations and actual arrivals, and even the likelihood of different classes of booking not arriving.

Finally an up-to-the-minute arrival list can be prepared and printed for distribution, although if the hotel has a number of VDUs in use then these can display the arrival list as required.

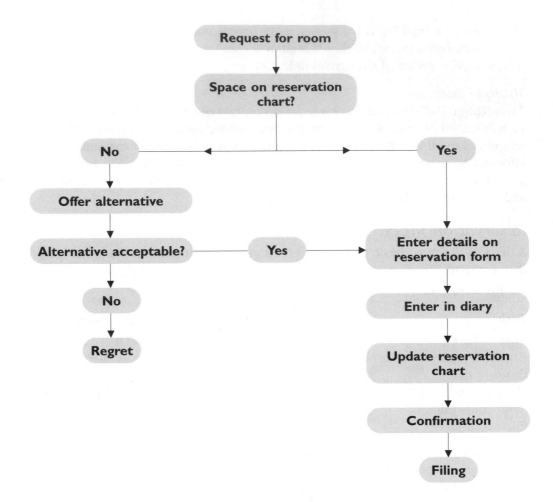

Fig. 4.4 *Reservation procedure.*

Charting reservations

It is necessary to make sure that there is a room available to sell, however a reservation is recorded. The position for any date in the future needs to be completely accurate. If it is overstated the request will be refused when space is available, and if all bookings are not recorded, then inadvertent overbooking may occur.

The booking chart has to be checked to establish whether or not it is possible to accept a reservation, or whether it has to be put on the waiting list or even refused.

The procedure for taking a booking is shown in Fig. 4.4. Once again, no matter how the request for a booking is received, the reservation clerk will have to follow through each step of the procedure.

All reservation charts follow the principle of showing the number of 'room nights' that are available in the hotel. This is done for each specific room on a 'conventional chart', or for groups of rooms on a 'density chart'.

Conventional chart

The conventional chart shows each room in the hotel individually. The room type is noted next to the room number. The chart is usually used in smaller hotels, where room types may differ substantially. It is particularly common in the older hotel which may have the following characteristics:

1 a great variety of room types;
2 a long average guest stay (three or more nights);
3 a long lead time of reservations;
4 some repeat business.

The chart functions by the receptionist allocating a room at the time of booking and noting this in the diary. An entry is made on the chart in pencil, with the name of the guest or a reference number by the booking. Weekends and bank holidays can be shown by shading (Fig. 4.5, overleaf).

1 entries must be made in pencil so that alterations can be made;
2 the arrows should run from the centre of each day as this corresponds with the hotel 'day' of midday;
3 if it is a short booking then the folio number from the diary should be used rather than the guest's name (e.g. Room 104 on 10th in Fig. 4.5);
4 chance bookings, extensions of stay, rooms off and early departures must be noted so that the chart is always accurate.

This form of chart is ideal for the smaller hotel, but it becomes difficult to see whether or not space is available as the hotel becomes full. Often a booking may be taken by 'juggling' the existing bookings. This means that an entry may be changed two or three times before guests actually arrive at the hotel and consequently, they are not informed of their room number until they actually register. A conventional chart can be very time-consuming to keep up-to-date, and errors often result in lower occupancy.

Density chart

Larger hotels use a density chart to record their bookings. With the density chart, rooms are classified into groups of a similar type and no allocation of a specific room is made until the guest arrives at the hotel. This is ideal for modern hotels where all rooms are similar, with only the floor level and view from the window changing. The density chart is also more useful where the guest stay is short, for entries can be made quickly and easily changed if necessary. As with the conventional chart, chance bookings, extensions, early departures, etc., all have to be noted on the chart to make sure it is a true picture of the reservation position. This is often checked by the reservations manager, who can compare the number of rooms let on the chart, with the actual number of guests in the hotel (and due to arrive) on a given day.

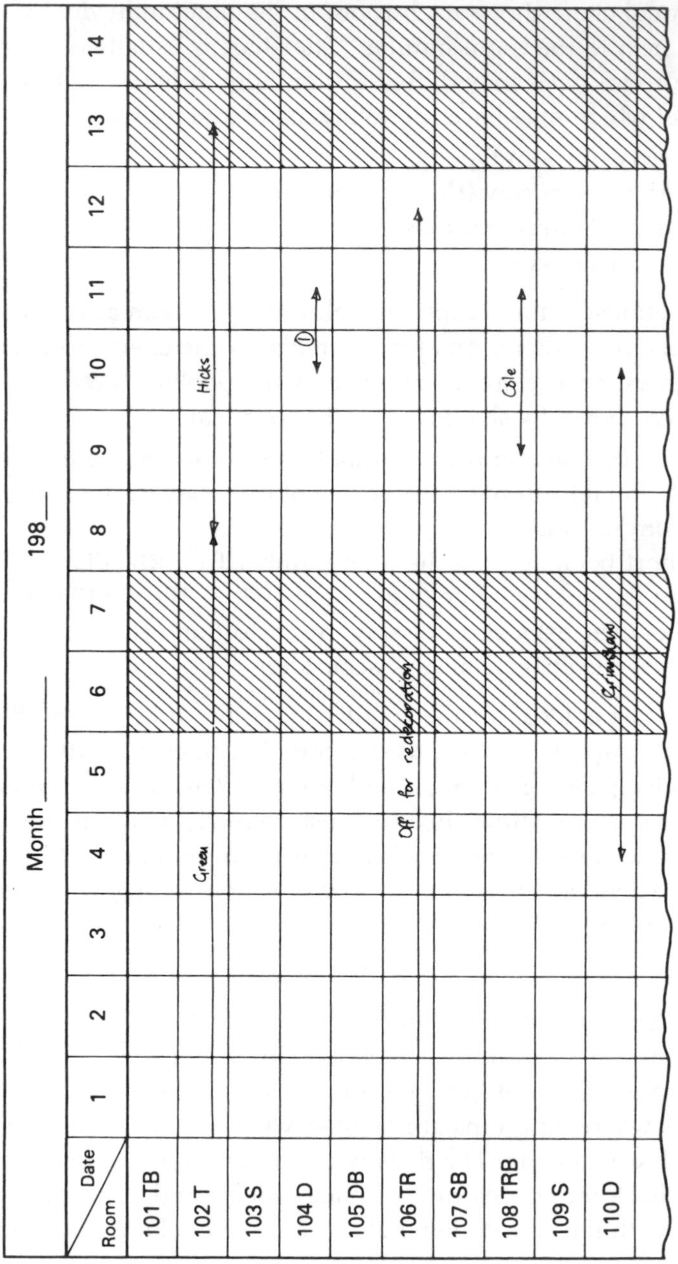

Month _____ 198__

Date / Room	1	2	3	4	5	6	7	8	9	10	11	12	13	14
101 TB														
102 T				Green						Hicks				
103 S														
104 D														
105 DB														
106 TR					Off for redecoration									
107 SB														
108 TRB										Cole				
109 S														
110 D						Crimson								

Fig. 4.5 Conventional reservation chart.

Density reservation chart

Figure 4.6 shows a density reservation chart in which each page represents one week and the pages are headed with the month and dates, and stored in a loose-leaf binder. Entries are made in pencil. Tours are entered quickly by

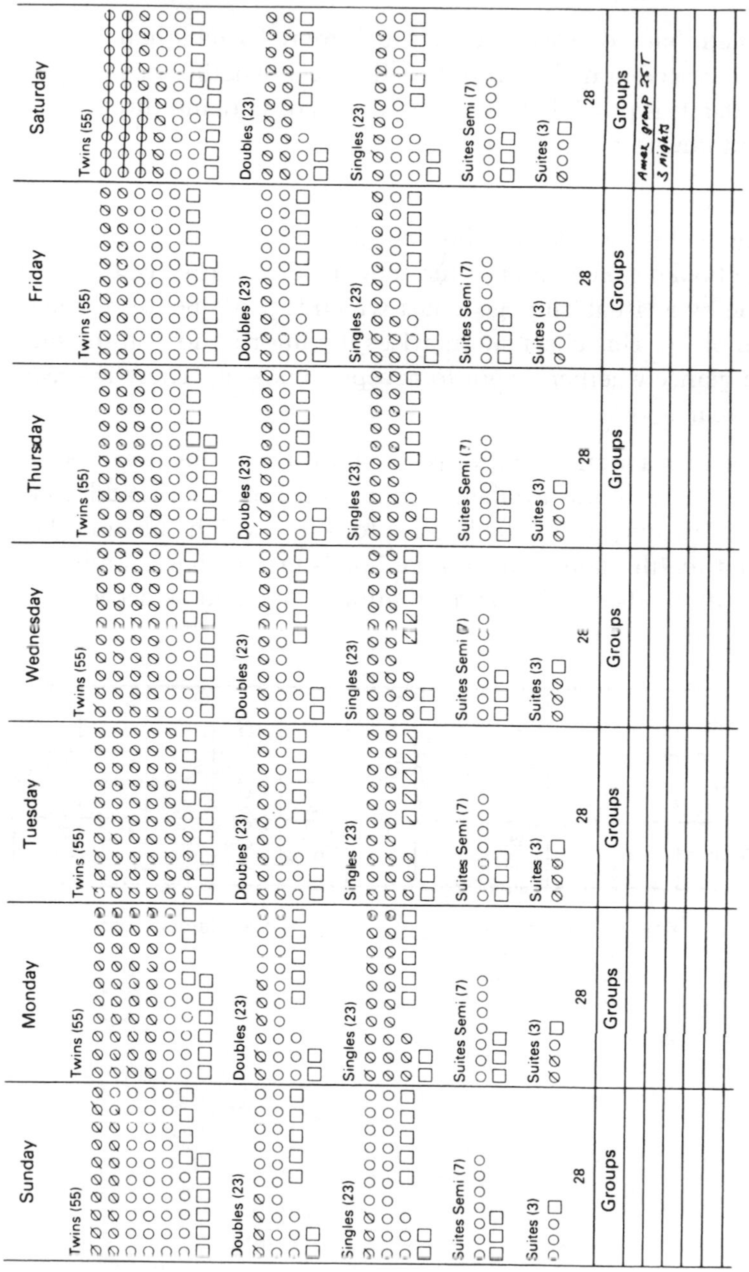

Fig. 4.6 Density reservation chart.

ruling off the appropriate number of rooms. The name of the tour is entered on the bottom line for quick reference. Each circle represents a 'room night'. The squares are for overbooking. There are 55 twin rooms in the hotel and allowance has been made for overbooking ten twins. (The total overbooking allowance is 28 rooms.)

It can be seen that a density chart is much more 'visual' than a conventional chart, and a reservation clerk could easily check whether or not space is available. Also it is possible to see the pattern of booking through the week by the 'ups and downs' of the reservations.

Stop–go chart

In large hotels there would be a bottleneck if every reservation clerk had to refer to the booking chart every time they handled a reservation request. This is overcome by a visual 'stop–go' chart which is prominently displayed in the reservation office. This chart summarises the information on the main chart. It shows at a glance whether or not to accept a booking. There is space for each day of the year.

Figure 4.7 shows a section of a stop–go chart. From this it can be seen that there are no single rooms available on 6th–8th June and in addition there are no twins on 7th June. It is fully booked for 4th and 5th July and there is a trade fair from 1st to 4th August. Most large hotels install charts similar to this in their reservation office and the information is updated as necessary by the reservations supervisor.

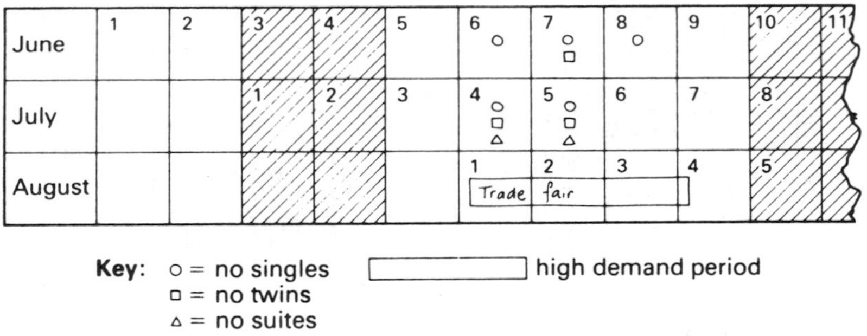

Key: o = no singles   [   ] high demand period
       □ = no twins
       ∆ = no suites

Fig. 4.7 *Part of a stop–go chart.*

Control of reservations

Close outs

A stop–go chart is an ideal method for the reservations supervisor to ensure maximum control of reservations. Some hotels will refuse bookings for a certain date even though they have rooms available. This helps the hotel to 'smooth' the booking pattern to ensure that occupancy is high every night.

The chart can be closed out by room type (i.e. no twins available on a particular date), or may be closed out by room type for arrivals only. This ensures that bookings will not be accepted for busy periods of one or two nights, but should an opportunity occur to secure a good booking, perhaps covering two weekends for example, it is possible to accept the reservation and 'book through' the busy period.

Alternatively, the reservations supervisor may estimate that the hotel will be able to fill all its accommodation for a particular period, and so aim to control reservations by closing out reduced rate business, ensuring that maximum revenue is earned for the time.

Yield management

Close outs are a crude example of yield management. Again airlines have developed the system to ensure that planes fly at the maximum profitability or 'yield'. Hotel yield management systems have developed as a separate add-on to normal reservation systems. They work by calculating how full the hotel is likely to be on a given date in the future. This is done by constantly measuring previous occupancy and booking patterns and projecting them forward into the future.

The reservationist is then 'advised' whether or not to take a booking, and at what rate. This has the effect of 'smoothing' peaks and troughs of demand and ensuring that rooms are sold at the best possible price. In a period of low demand, Sunday evening for example, the system would recommend accepting a rate lower than 'rack' to ensure the booking and gain revenue for the hotel. It should be recognised that the hotel room can never be sold twice. Like an airline or coach seat, it is perishable. If a room is not sold on a particular night then it is never sold. This is because there are two elements: **space** (the room) and **time** (the date). The effect this has upon sales and profitability is looked at in Chapters 9 and 10.

Overbooking

Overbooking is the practice of accepting more reservations than there is space available. The purpose of overbooking is to assist the hotel in obtaining maximum occupancy, and to compensate for early departures, last-minute cancellations and non-arrivals. On the density chart (Fig. 4.6), overbooking was allowed to 25%. For most hotels this is a high figure. The reception department should keep figures of non-arrivals and early departures, and from these should calculate the percentage to which overbooking is possible. In this way, overbooking becomes a way of controlling reservations by booking to a predetermined number of rooms based on the anticipated non-arrivals for that date. Viewed in this way, overbooking becomes good sales technique, rather than sloppy and unprofessional practice.

The degree of overbooking will vary not only from one hotel to another but also from week to week and day to day in the same hotel.

Reservations departments that are operating on a computer system will usually find that the system will record the relationship between reservations and actual arrivals, and even the likelihood of different classes of booking not arriving. Obviously this is a great boon to the hotel, and should ensure that serious overbooking never occurs.

A hotel with a highly transient trade will be able to overbook more than a hotel in a resort where guests book three months in advance and stay for two-week periods. The fact that a hotel overbooks does not mean that it will have to refuse guests rooms. The aim of overbooking is to balance exactly the extra rooms booked with the non-arrivals and cancellations. Only if this goes wrong is it necessary to 'book out' guests to another hotel. A middle way is to accept bookings on a waiting list for cancellations.

Confirming reservations

Many hotels send a letter of confirmation to people who make reservations. This serves a number of purposes. It can be evidence of a contract. The law is in favour of the person booking the room. A contract exists when the guest posts the letter of confirmation, and can only be cancelled by the hotel when the guest receives the letter withdrawing the previous offer. If the guest is not accommodated, then he or she may be able to sue for material loss as a result of the breaking of the contract. In certain states in the USA, guests are able to sue for 'disturbance' if they are not accommodated by the hotel at which they booked.

Standard confirmations

All reservation systems will print a confirmation if required. Fewer and fewer guests expect them nowadays. They are particularly useful if there are details that the guest needs to be made aware of. Examples include the following:

- deposit request
- cancellation periods
- arrival times and release time

Deposits and guarantees

Most hotels operate a system of asking for one night's payment for each room as a deposit, a guarantee on a credit card or a guarantee from the booking company. In this way the room can be held all night for the guest to arrive without the risk of losing revenue.

Length of stay deposits

In particularly busy and high demand locations, a hotel may tell the guest that the deposit will be used against a room charge for early departure. So, if a guest books for five days, but actually leaves after three, the hotel may charge the deposit as an early departure penalty.

In the US, some hotels will charge an early departure fee of, say, $50. This again is linked to the sophisticated yield management system, which would have quoted the guest a rate based upon the length of stay.

Cancellation

If a guest cancels the booking, then the reservation procedure has to be reversed; the booking is crossed through in the diary, the chart entry is erased and the details are married together in the files. The hotel may sue the guest for loss if the guest cancels the booking, but the hotel must make every attempt to re-let the accommodation, and can only claim for the actual loss incurred.

When a computerised system is in use a cancellation may continue to be displayed on the screen but be clearly marked as cancelled. In the case of amended arrival dates it may be particularly helpful to refer to previous information. If a guest cancels a booking for the week beginning 7th June and the hotel is able to re-let the accommodation for the last three nights of the week, a claim can only be made for the first four nights of the booking rather than the whole week. To claim for the whole week would be equal to selling the room twice.

While some seasonal hotels press claims for compensation when a guest cancels at short notice, it is very rare for city centre hotels to do so. Obviously this may vary if a tour cancels at very short notice, and the hotel has no chance of re-letting the accommodation, but this is normally covered by the terms of a special contract between the hotel and the tour operator.

Filing reservations

The various bookings are kept in arrival date order and brought forward to the front desk for each day's arrival. In the event of a query the receptionist can then check the details easily. Multiple arrival dates are dealt with by photocopying the letter for each arrival date and filing accordingly.

Status of reservations

6 p.m. release

Reservations are often taken on the basis that the guest will arrive by a certain time of day. If they arrive before that time they have their room in the normal way. If they arrive after the time they have to take a chance on a room being available when they arrive. This enables the hotel to be certain it is full, without the risk of having to charge guests for non-arrival if they are delayed or change their plans.

Guaranteed arrival

This is the reverse of a 6 p.m. release. Here the guests guarantee to pay for the room whether they arrive or not. It is very useful for guests who may be arriving late at night, or even early the next morning from a transatlantic flight. Guaranteed arrival facilities are normally offered only to companies, or travel agents, who the hotel can be certain will honour their commitments.

Take or place (T or P)

Regular customers are often offered a 'take or place' booking if they reserve at short notice. When they arrive at the hotel a room will be allocated to them if there has been a cancellation. If there has not been any cancellation or non-arrival, then the hotel will find another room for them in a comparable hotel. This facility is often offered by chain hotels, for while one hotel in the group may be full, there may be vacancies elsewhere. This 'T or P' facility helps to retain customer loyalty and also maximises occupancy for individual hotels or groups.

Tours and groups

Each hotel will have its own definition of a tour, some specifying that any booking of more than five rooms shall be treated as a 'group'. Special procedures are generally followed for these reservations and any deposits that may be paid. These are explained fully in Chapter 10.

Commissionable bookings

Reservations made by travel agents and hotel booking agents are normally subject to a commission payment to the agent on the room rate. This fact is noted in the remarks column of the diary, so that the bill can be marked as commissionable when the guest checks in. Frequently two bills may be opened: one for the apartment charge showing the appropriate commission, and a second bill for any extras incurred by the guest. This ensures that the commission is only deducted from the accommodation charge.

Assignment

You are working in a 200-room luxury hotel in a capital city. Prepare a flow chart showing the questions a reservations clerk should ask when taking a telephone reservation. Produce a supplementary list of questions designed to increase sales.

CHAPTER 5

Checking in and Staying

After studying this chapter you should be able to

- describe the various methods of registering guests
- outline the key legal requirement concerning registration and keeping the records
- show how the hotel communicates the information to other departments
- understand how guest history preferences are dealt with

Registration

There is a legal obligation for a hotel to obtain, and keep for twelve months, certain information about every person who stays there. The basic requirement is full name and nationality. If the guest is from overseas, then they have to provide, in addition, their passport number and place of issue, their next destination and the address there, if known. A guest staying at a hotel need not in law provide their true name, but obviously the hotel would view with caution anyone they thought was not using their true name.

In addition to this legal minimum, hotels request further information from guests who stay with them. A home address and signature are asked for in all hotels. Others take the opportunity to find out more about their customers by asking for information such as car registration number, purpose of visit, occupation, proposed method of payment, and other details.

These requests can be placed into two categories: administrative, to ensure the smooth efficient running of the operation; and marketing, where the hotel takes the opportunity to find out more about its customers' habits.

Date	Family name	Other names	Full address	Signature	Room	Nationality
23/6	Sparrow	George	11 Field Lane Warmington	C. Sparrow	321	British
23/6	Finch	Clive	27 Fowlers Walk, Ealing	C. Finch	709	U. K
23/6	Finch	Janet	27 Fowlers Walk Ealing W5	J. Finch	709	U. K.

Fig. 5.1 *Specimen page of a register.*

OVERSEAS VISITORS

Family name _Corbeau_   Other names _Charles_

Passport no. _XY 12345_   Place of _Paris_
issue

Nationality _French_   Next destination _Oxford_

Date _23/6_   _____

Fig. 5.2 *Aliens form.*

Register

The traditional method of checking guests in is to use a register. This is a large, bound book ruled into columns which the guest fills out upon arrival. It is ideal for smaller hotels where guests arrive individually. A register provides a permanent record of guests staying in the hotel; it is unlikely to be lost, and guests are recorded in chronological order. The cost per guest is also very low, for each guest will take up only one line of the register. A typical register is shown in Fig. 5.1.

Overseas guests are normally asked to fill out a supplementary 'aliens form' to provide the additional information that is required (Fig. 5.2).

The register suffers from some disadvantages. If more than one guest wishes to check in there is a waiting time; in the case of a tour this time could be considerable. Also, the receptionist is unable to process registration information while a guest is checking in, so administration delays could occur in notifying other departments, and opening the bill. As each guest individually registers, there may be entries made in the wrong column which need to be crossed out. Handwriting and inks will differ, and the overall effect becomes rather untidy. More importantly, it is an indiscreet method in that it provides guests with the opportunity to find out information about other people staying at the hotel.

Loose-leaf registers are now available, which overcomes some of the disadvantages.

Registration cards

The majority of hotels now use registration cards (Fig. 5.3). These overcome the problems and bottlenecks of a register. Naturally they are more expensive, but they have many benefits. After departure they can be filed in alphabetical order and they are easy to copy on a photocopier.

Different properties will tailor the card to their particular needs. Motels will seek car registration numbers. Airport hotels may look for airline flight details and so on.

Holiday Inn Garden Court — Owned by C.R.D. Catering (City) Ltd and operated under licence from Holiday Inns, Inc.	GUEST REGISTRATION — ROOM NUMBER		
NAME	ARR. DATE	DEP. DATE	NIGHTS
COMPANY ADDRESS	PERSONS	ROOM TYPE	RATE
		BOOKING	DEPOSIT
HOME ADDRESS	I WISH TO SETTLE MY ACCOUNT BY:- ☐ CASH ☐ CHEQUE (only to the value of a Bankers Card) ☐ CREDIT CARD TYPE _____ NUMBER _____ EXP. DATE: _____ ☐ AUTHORISED ACCOUNT TO COMPANY		
PRIORITY CLUB No.	☐ VOUCHER		
NATIONALITY	CAR REGISTRATION NO.	SIGNATURE	
FOR OUR OVERSEAS GUESTS			
NEXT DESTINATION	COUNTRY OF RESIDENCE	I agree that my liability for this account is not waived and I agree to be held personally liable in the event that the indicated person, company or association fails to pay all or part of these charges.	
PASSPORT NUMBER	ISSUED AT	REFERENCE	S/LDR

Fig. 5.3 *Registration card suitable for computer printing.*

A computerised system will normally print the registration card from the reservation details. This saves time for the guest on arrival. All the guest has to do is sign and complete the missing sections.

Even in the most modern systems the guest is still usually asked to sign – without a signature it would be difficult to prove that charges had been incurred, and there would be no proof of the guest's stay. This is particularly important when the account is sent to a company for payment. A computer may also be programmed with details of any undesirable guests who may have caused problems in the past, or been 'blacklisted'.

Checking

The receptionist should always check the registration card or register once the guest has checked in. It is then possible to make sure that the card has been completed correctly and that the information is legible. If there is a query the receptionist can politely ask the guest for clarification and enter the details. This is particularly important with some nationalities where it is not immediately apparent which name is the surname.

It is also important to check that the reservation details are still the same. The receptionist can then inform the guest of the room number and room rate. By telling the guest the rate, the receptionist is complying with the law and avoiding potential difficulties at check-out, when there may be a rate query. Additionally the receptionist may ascertain at this point how the guest will make payment for the stay. To summarise, registering the guest is probably one of the most important tasks assigned to a receptionist. In addition to being polite and putting the guest at their ease, there are a number of checks to be made:

1   that the registration details are correct and legible;
2   that the details of the booking have not changed;
3   that the guest knows the room rate and what it includes;
4   how the guest intends to pay;
5   whether there are any letters or messages for the guest;
6   that the room is ready;
7   that sales techniques have been used to maximum effect.

Booking out

The chapter on reservations explained the principle and aims of overbooking. When a mistake is made in the amount of overbooking, it is necessary to send some arrivals to another hotel, because there is no space for them. The first stage in handling the situation is to ensure that the arrival list is absolutely correct, that there are no entries that have been cancelled, or switched to another date or entered twice. The reception manager can then establish the exact number of guests it will be necessary to book out. At the same time, a check can be made to ascertain the length of time the hotel is overbooked for: is it one night, two nights or longer? All arrivals due can be classified into six groups according to their booking source:

1   UK individuals
2   overseas individuals
3   UK companies
4   overseas companies
5   UK travel agents
6   overseas travel agents

From these groups should be removed all VIPs and CIPs who are to be given priority in room allocation. The residue will comprise the people who can be booked out. The aim of the hotel in overbooking in the first place was to maximise income, so in booking out guests it is important to choose people who, if offended, have the least effect upon the business in the long term. Therefore, it is preferable to book out a guest from overseas who is unlikely to return, rather than a guest booked by the hotel's largest business house user.

Normally the hotel will reserve alternative accommodation for the guest in a hotel that is at least as good, and pay all the out-of-pocket expenses of the guest, taxi fares, telephone calls, etc. If the hotel is in a group then if at all possible another group hotel is used. Telephone and other guest-contact departments are notified of the hotel into which the guest has been re-booked: in this way all messages will be passed on as quickly as possible.

Any guest who is booked out will have a genuine grievance against the hotel, and will probably complain vehemently; for this reason the actual handling of the booking out is best done by the senior receptionist on duty, or the assistant manager.

Compensation
Following the lead of airlines, who regularly overbook flights, some chain hotels have a rule of operation that compensates the guest for being booked out. This can either be vouchers for a subsequent stay, or the cost of one night at the alternative property. Even after meeting these compensation costs it is still in the interests of the hotel to overbook by a sensible margin to achieve the objective of a 'full house'.

Chance arrivals
A guest who stays at the hotel without a prior booking is often referred to as a 'chance' guest. 'Transient' hotels will receive the bulk of their guests as chance arrivals.

The receptionist has less information about the potential guest and their credit-worthiness in this situation, so special procedures are adopted to handle their bookings.

Chance arrivals with substantial amounts of luggage are unlikely to be able to leave the hotel without paying, for their departure would be noticed by a member of staff. An increasing trend, however, is the carrying of small amounts of luggage, which means the guest may be able to leave unnoticed. In registering the guest, the receptionist first checks whether they have luggage; if they do, then the registration is processed in the normal way and the registration card is marked 'Chance'.

If there is little or no luggage, then the receptionist has to ensure that the guest will not leave without first settling their bill. This can be done either by taking a cash deposit from the guest, or alternatively by taking an imprint of any credit card that the guest may have. Certainly, in registering a chance guest it is essential that some corroboration of the details of the registration card is obtained. Obviously, it is important that in accepting chance bookings and taking deposits, the receptionist does not suggest to the guest that the hotel thinks they may be dishonest, or not willing to pay. Chance guests are often asked to pay cash for all purchases while they are in the hotel, or alternatively, a special check may be kept on the size of their bill, so that if the account exceeds a set figure (say £100) the guest is contacted and asked to pay up to that date. By doing this, potential losses from chance guests are minimised.

Again the computerised hotel will find it easier. On check-in, the receptionist will be offered the option of authorising charges to that room. For a chance guest without a credit card, the receptionist may choose to bar the telephones, mini bar, pay movies, and bar and restaurant charge facilities so that the guest has to pay cash in all these departments.

No trace reservations

Even in the most efficient office there will be an occasion when a guest arrives to check in and there is no trace of the reservation. This can occur for a variety of reasons but the remedy is nearly always the same – the guest must be asked for details of the booking. This must be done as discreetly as possible and then all the records must be checked. The reservation may have been listed under the company name, or the name of the person who made the booking. It is also possible that the guest made two bookings at once, and one of them may have been overlooked, or has not been cross-referenced.

After the correspondence has been checked and an exhaustive search made, normal arrival procedures should be adopted. Remember, if the client is unknown to you the booking should be treated as if it were chance – an excellent opportunity to demonstrate social skills.

Key card

Some hotels give a key card to their guests when they check in (Figs 5.4 and 5.5). This is either a card or small booklet which has the guest's name, room number and room rate on it. Inside there are details of the restaurants and other hotel facilities. Often this is linked with advertising for local shops and services and may then be self-financing. Key cards can be printed in different colours to indicate the different status of guests. A red key card, for example, would identify a chance guest, who would then be asked to pay cash for all house purchases. A key card fulfils three separate functions:

1   it can be used as a security check when guests collect their keys;
2   it advertises facilities both in and out of the hotel;
3   it satisfies the obligation to inform guests of their room rate when they register.

The key card can provide a useful function upon departure. Should a guest query their departure date, or their rate, the receptionist can refer the guest to their key card for the details – assuming it is correct. Many systems will print the key card at the same time as the registration card (Fig. 5.6, page 95).

The key card is given to the guest by the receptionist and shows that the check-in procedure is almost complete.

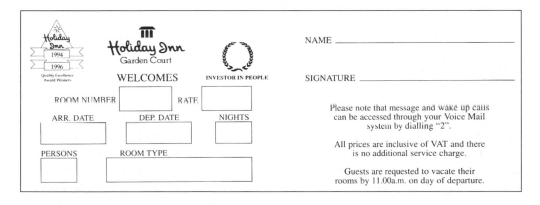

Fig. 5.4   *A chain hotel key card.*

Front

Holiday Inn
CROWNE PLAZA®
KÖLN

HABSBURGERRING 9 - 13 · 50674 KÖLN
TELEFON (02 21) 20 95 - 0
TELEFAX (02 21) 25 12 06

Name/
Name/_____ *Mr Dix*

Zimmernummer/
Room number/_____ *406*

Zimmerpreis/
Room rate/_____ *£6 ex*

Abreise-Datum/
Departure date/_____

Kostenfreie Stornierung nicht möglich.
Cancellation free of charge not possible.

ABREISEZEIT: 13 UHR
CHECK OUT TIME: 1 p.m.

Wertsachen
Die Haftung erfolgt nach den gesetzlichen Bestimmungen.
Die Direktion ist nicht verantwortlich für Verluste von Geld
und Wertsachen. Bitte benutzen Sie unsere Schließfächer, die
am Empfang frei zur Verfügung stehen.

Valuables
The Liability is according to the laws of the Federal Republic
of Germany.
Management is not responsible for any loss of money or
valuables in your room. Please use safe deposit boxes kept at
your disposal free of charge at our front-office.

Back

LE BOUQUET

1. Stock/first floor, Telefon: 168
6.30 - 23.00 Uhr / 6.30 a.m. - 11.00 p.m.

LOBBY BAR

Erdgeschoß/groundfloor, Telefon: 543
täglich 8.00 - 18.00 Uhr
sonntags 8.00 -24.00 Uhr
daily from 8.00 a.m. - 6.00 p.m.
on sundays 8.00 a.m. - 12.00 p.m.

St GEORGES

Erdgeschoß/groundfloor, Telefon: 570
18.00 - 1.00 Uhr / 6.00 p.m. - 1.00 a.m.
außer sonn- und feiertags
except sundays and holidays

Fig. 5.5 *A handwritten key card.*

Keys

The key itself may not be kept at reception since in the larger hotels it will
almost certainly be held by the porters or at the information desk. Keys are
usually kept on a large tag to prevent clients from taking them away (either
intentionally or by accident). The tag is usually marked with the room number
and the name of the hotel to facilitate return should it be taken away, and is
consequently a big security problem.

Holiday Inn Garden Court — Owned by C.R.D. Catering (City) Ltd and operated under licence from Holiday Inns, Inc.

GUEST REGISTRATION — ROOM NUMBER

NAME	ARR. DATE	DEP. DATE	NIGHTS
COMPANY ADDRESS	PERSONS	ROOM TYPE	RATE
		BOOKING	DEPOSIT
HOME ADDRESS	I WISH TO SETTLE MY ACCOUNT BY:-		
	☐ CASH ☐ CHEQUE (only to the value of a Bankers Card)		
	☐ CREDIT CARD TYPE ____ NUMBER ____ EXP. DATE: ____		
	☐ AUTHORISED ACCOUNT TO COMPANY		
PRIORITY CLUB No.	☐ VOUCHER		

NATIONALITY	CAR REGISTRATION NO.	SIGNATURE	
FOR OUR OVERSEAS GUESTS			
NEXT DESTINATION	COUNTRY OF RESIDENCE	I agree that my liability for this account is not waived and I agree to be held personally liable in the event that the indicated person, company or association fails to pay all or part of these charges.	
PASSPORT NUMBER	ISSUED AT	REFERENCE	S/LDR

Holiday Inn 1994 1996 Quality Excellence Award Winners

Holiday Inn Garden Court WELCOMES

INVESTOR IN PEOPLE

ROOM NUMBER ____ RATE ____

ARR. DATE ____ DEP. DATE ____ NIGHTS ____

PERSONS ____ ROOM TYPE ____

NAME ____

SIGNATURE ____

Please note that message and wake up calls can be accessed through your Voice Mail system by dialling "2".

All prices are inclusive of VAT and there is no additional service charge.

Guests are requested to vacate their rooms by 11.00a.m. on day of departure.

Fig. 5.6 *Registration card key card printed together.*

The credit-card-sized electronic key is not normally handed in by the guest each time they leave the hotel; they simply keep it with them. The key can be used for showing the hotel logo (Fig. 5.7, overleaf) – or some hotels sell advertising space, perhaps for a night club or department store.

Fig. 5.7 *A guest key with the hotel logo.*

Room status

A prime need for every hotel is an accurate, up-to-date knowledge of the state of every room in the hotel. A room can be in one of four states:

1 let
2 vacant and not ready
3 vacant and ready
4 closed for repair or decoration

A room status system must be able to show these four positions and be capable of being quickly changed. Systems adopted range from the very simple manual system that will operate in a small hotel to computerised systems that carry out a number of management functions in large city centre hotels.

Bedroom book

The bedroom book is the most basic system. It is operated entirely manually and requires a large amount of clerical work. However, because it is generally used in hotels of less than 20 rooms, this is not too demanding.

The bedroom book is normally a diary that has a page for each day. A line is ruled for each day, for every room in the hotel. As the guest registers, their

Monday 10th June	Tuesday 11th June
10 T Finch, Mr/s J £15	10 T Finch, Mr/s J £15
11 T B	11 T B
12 S Sparrow, Mr. H. £8	12 S
14 D	14 D
15 DB	15 DB

Fig. 5.8 *Entries in a bedroom book.*

name is written next to the room number on the page of the arrival day, and is rewritten for each day that they stay. So, if a guest books for fourteen nights, their name is written on fourteen pages of the bedroom book. From Fig. 5.8 it can be seen that room 10 is occupied by Mr and Mrs J. Finch on 10th and 11th June, and that they are paying a rate of £15 per night.

Next to room numbers are the room types. On 10th June, room 12 is occupied by Mr H. Sparrow, but he is due to check out on 11th. There has to be a method of showing that a room has been occupied overnight, or a receptionist may send an arrival to room 12 before the guest has left, or before it is ready. A common way of doing this is to use three sides of a triangle to show the state of the room:

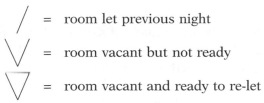

/ = room let previous night

∨ = room vacant but not ready

▽ = room vacant and ready to re-let

As with the reservation chart, if guests leave early or extend their stay the receptionist has to update the bedroom book accordingly. This applies to all the room status systems. Individual hotels modify this system to their own needs in many different ways, but in all cases it has the advantage of providing a permanent record of room status. Figure 5.8 also shows that the room numbers are 10, 11, 12, 14, 15. There is no room 13. Many hotels avoid numbering a room 13, to avoid incidents with superstitious guests. This is also the case in larger hotels, where there is rarely a floor numbered 13.

Bed sheet

The bed sheet or room-letting sheet is a development of the bedroom book and is often used in hotels of up to 100 rooms, which are not computerised. The information is recorded onto a sheet pre-printed with room numbers, types and three sections. One sheet is used for each day, and the day and date are entered by the receptionist. During the evening shift, the entries are copied over onto the sheet for the next day.

Figure 5.9 shows the three-section bed sheet for 11th June. Guests are entered into the appropriate column depending on whether they are arriving, staying or leaving. A guest who was booked for only one night would move straight from the arrivals column to the departures. This three-column system is very effective, for it enables the receptionist to see quickly the rooms that will be available to let that day. It is also possible to allocate rooms before guests have checked out.

In the example (Fig. 5.9) of 11th June, it can be seen that Mr Dove in Room 102 is staying until 20th June. Room 103 is being vacated by Mr and Mrs Jay, and the receptionist has allocated the room to Mr and Mrs Raven. In completing the sheet, the receptionist would write the room allocations in pencil, so that changes can be easily made. When the guests arrive and have registered, then the details can be entered in ink in the arrival column. During the evening shift the receptionist will copy over the details of each room from the sheet of one day to the new sheet. Thus, in the example, Mr and Mrs Raven would be entered into the 'staying' column of the bed sheet of 12th June. It is still necessary to show whether or not the departure has been made, and also whether or not the room has ben cleaned and returned by the housekeeping department.

Room board

A room board is used in larger hotels. The board is made of slots located next to each room number (Fig. 5.10, page 100). As each guest registers, a small card is filled out with details of the guest and the length of stay and this is placed into the appropriate room slot. When the guest checks out, the card is removed and thrown away. With this system, there is much less clerical work, for the guest's name is written only once. Coloured cards can be used to show whether or not a room is ready to be occupied. A room board is a quick, visual guide to room status, but unlike the previous two systems, it does not provide a permanent record.

Day Tuesday   Date 11th June

Room	Arrivals				Staying				Departures			
	Name	Sleepers	Rate	Dep.	Name	Sleepers	Rate	Dep.	Name	Sleepers	Rate	Dep.
101 TB												
102 SB					Dove	1	£20	20/6				
103 D	Raven	2	£30	13/6					Jay	2	£20	11/6
104 TRB												
105 DB												
106 S	← Off for re-decoration →											

Fig. 5.9 Part of a bed sheet.

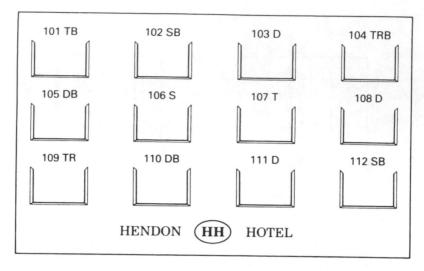

Fig. 5.10   *Part of a room board.*

Room status boards

A room status system (e.g. Whitney) is simply a development of the room board. Although some of the components are interchangeable with the advance reservation rack system, they do not have to be used together. The rack is for the whole hotel, with a slot for each room. The rack is tailor-made for each hotel. In some systems there is a perspex slider which can be in one of three positions relating to the colours clear, red or yellow. The room type is shown in the centre of each slot, and the room types are colour-coded over the room numbers on the left. In this way, the room type can be identified even when a rack slip is in place. Arrows are used to show communicating rooms. The centre section can also be used to show the room rate and the location of each room (Fig. 5.11). With this method, the maximum information about the room is presented to the receptionist.

The three colours of the perspex slider can be used to show the current state of the room (Fig. 5.11):

- red   =   room vacant but not ready;
- clear   =   room vacant and ready;
- yellow =   room just let.

The advantage of a room status board such as this is that more than one receptionist can register guests and allocate rooms instantly, minimising the risk of two people being given the same room.

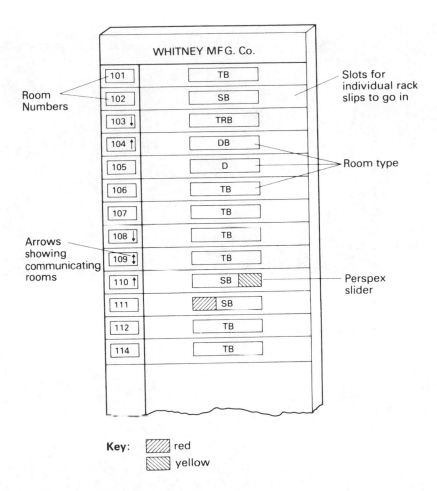

Fig. 5.11 *Part of a room status rack.*

In many of these systems, information relating to the guest is entered onto a carbonated rack slip, the top copy of which is placed in the room slot until the guest checks out. The other copies may be used by other departments (such as porters and switchboard) to make an alphabetical display of guests currently in the hotel.

When a guest checks out, the rack slip is removed from the room slot, and can then be crossed through to show the guest has left, and distributed to other departments. This allows departure to be noted as swiftly as arrival; all that is required of staff is to remove the slip of the guest who has left and dispose of it.

This important task of circulating the arrival and departure notifications will ensure that all departments are able to keep their house lists in order.

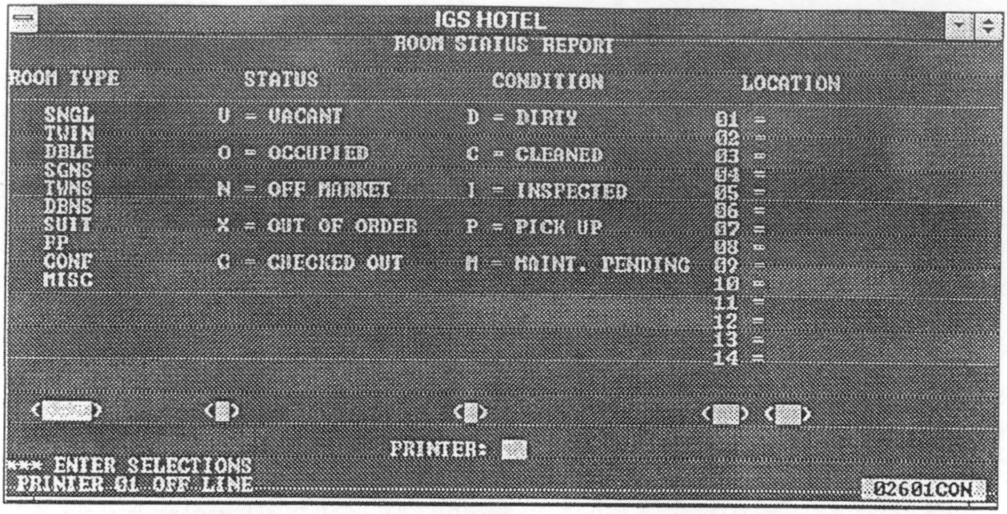

IGS HOTEL

ROOM STATUS REPORT

ROOM TYPE	STATUS	CONDITION	LOCATION
SNGL	U = VACANT	D = DIRTY	01 =
TWIN			02 =
DBLE	O = OCCUPIED	C = CLEANED	03 =
SGNS			04 =
TWNS	N = OFF MARKET	I = INSPECTED	05 =
DBNS			06 =
SUIT	X = OUT OF ORDER	P = PICK UP	07 =
PP			08 =
CONF	C = CHECKED OUT	M = MAINT. PENDING	09 =
MISC			10 =
			11 =
			12 =
			13 =
			14 =

PRINTER:

*** ENTER SELECTIONS
PRINTER 01 OFF LINE   02601CON

Fig. 5.12 *Room status front screen.*

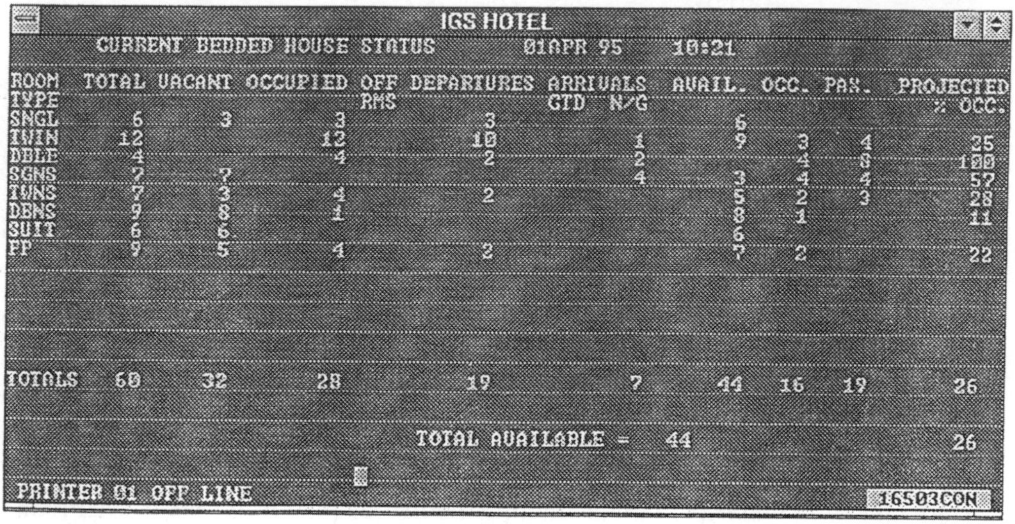

IGS HOTEL

CURRENT BEDDED HOUSE STATUS   01APR 95   10:21

ROOM TYPE	TOTAL	VACANT	OCCUPIED	OFF RMS	DEPARTURES	ARRIVALS GTD	N/G	AVAIL.	OCC.	PAX.	PROJECTED % OCC.
SNGL	6	3	3		3			6			
TWIN	12		12		10	1		9	3	4	25
DBLE	4		4		2	2			4	8	100
SGNS	2	2				4		3	4	4	57
TWNS	7	3	4		2			5	2	3	28
DBNS	9	8	1					8	1		11
SUIT	6	6						6			
PP	9	5	4		2			7	2		22
TOTALS	60	32	28		19	7		44	16	19	26

TOTAL AVAILABLE = 44   26

PRINTER 01 OFF LINE   16503CON

Fig. 5.13 *Current room status screen.*

Computer

Room status handled by computer is accurate, and both easily and quickly displayed (Figs 5.12 and 5.13). Details of each room are stored within the memory, and as a guest registers the guest list is immediately updated, while that particular room is removed from the list of those which are available for letting. Because the system is so accurate there is little chance of two people being given the same room.

Information on guests' rooms is automatically transferred to all terminals throughout the hotel. This will include the switchboard, so calls can be put through to guests as they reach their room. The computer can present this information either alphabetically or by room number.

Room allocation

When the guests arrive they will want to be able to use their rooms as quickly as possible. If they arrive before midday, then it is unlikely that the rooms will be ready unless they are vacant from the previous night. In smaller hotels allocation of rooms is normally done at the time of booking, by using the conventional chart. If when a guest arrives the room allocated is not ready, but a similar one is, then the chart has to be changed round to show the re-allocation. Larger hotels with a greater choice of rooms often do not allocate until the guest actually arrives, and then place the guest in the room of the type required that is ready. VIPs and guests with special requirements may have rooms pre-allocated to them and a note may be placed in the reception area to ensure that they only go to those particular rooms.

In allocating rooms the receptionist should aim to satisfy the guests as much as possible. Even in large modern hotels not every room is exactly the same; some may have better views than others, and certain rooms may be particularly noisy due to their proximity to the lift or a service pantry. Allocation should take place on the basis of putting the guests who are staying the longest into the best rooms at their rate, and guests who booked first into rooms better than those guests who booked at the last moment or are chance arrivals. By following this strategy the rooms in the hotel that are the least satisfactory will always be the last to be let. Out of season, some hotels let only sections of the hotel so that whole floors may be closed down, either for cleaning, or to save unnecessary lighting and heat.

A hotel which operates a computerised system will ensure that the program carries provision for different tariffs, locations and individual guest preferences. The computer will select the best available room for a particular reservation, or offer alternatives if the preferred room is already taken or not yet ready. It is essential that the program is flexible enough to ensure that any special requests by guests can be catered for.

Notifications and records

A system of departmental notifications and records has to be kept to ensure that the needs of the guest (and management) are satisfied. In a hotel where a computer is in use these notifications and records pose no problem at all.

A sensible method of distribution would be to ensure the placing of a VDU in all relevant departments. This would enable the arrival and departure situation to be updated instantly, and room changes recorded without tedious paperwork. Additionally, the other departments could request information from the computer if required, and save themselves time and trouble.

Many hotels, however, still rely on traditional methods of notification to other departments.

Arrival list

Normally one day in advance, an alphabetical arrival list is prepared showing all guests due to arrive, their length of stay and any special requirements they may have. This list will be useful to both the porter and the telephonist. The porter or enquiry desk will wish to check whether there are any messages or letters for guests arriving, and the telephonist may answer enquiries from people about the arrival of particular guests. Tour members or conference delegates are normally listed separately under the name of the booking agent. The reception desk will be able to use the alphabetical list to locate guests quickly in the diary.

Departmental notifications

Individual arrival notifications are rarely used now, although a rack slip serves the same purpose. When a tour has arrived, and the rooms have been allocated, a tour list is passed to each department as soon as possible so that queries can be answered.

Moves from one room to another require an individual notification because the records of each department need to be updated. A typical move notification is shown in Fig. 5.14.

House list

An alphabetical guest list is usually prepared each evening by the reception department. This is then distributed throughout the hotel, though some departments may only check it occasionally. The telephone department, porter's desk and reception will need to refer to it constantly, but there is little need for the kitchen to receive a copy. A list of guests in room number order is only kept

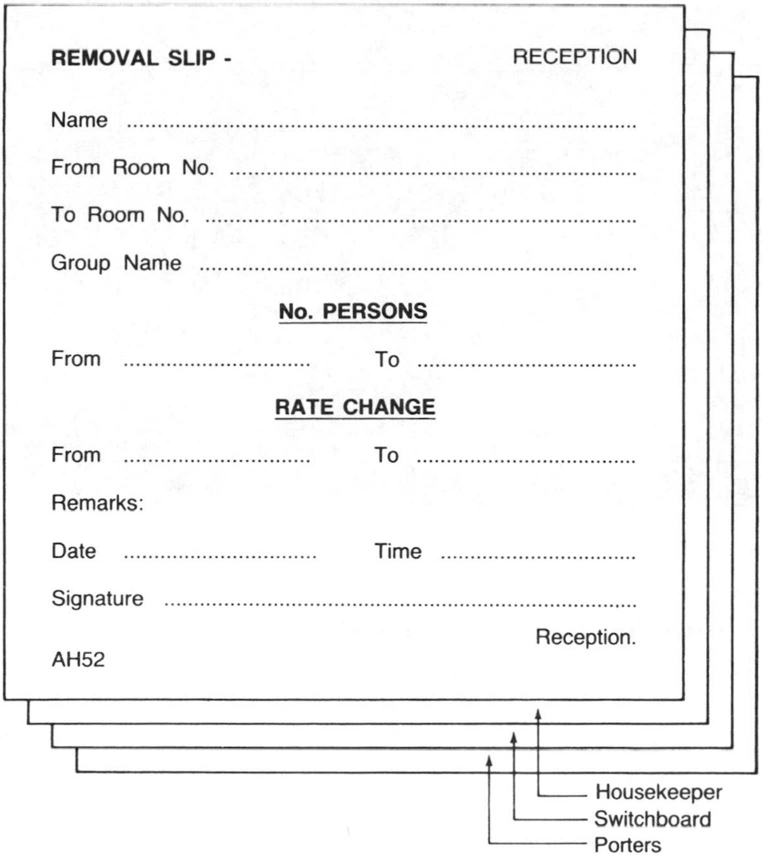
REMOVAL SLIP - RECEPTION

Name ....

From Room No. ....

To Room No. ....

Group Name ....

No. PERSONS

From .... To ....

RATE CHANGE

From .... To ....

Remarks:

Date .... Time ....

Signature ....

Reception.

AH52

Fig. 5.14 *Move notification.*

at the reception through the room board, or bed sheet, and anyone wishing to know who is in a particular room would have to check with the reception desk. For many 'transient' hotels the house list is only an approximation for as soon as it is distributed the position will change due to the departure of some guests and the arrival of others.

Departure list

The departure list is prepared in room number order and is often combined with the house list for circulation to all departments of the hotel. Work allocation by the housekeeping department will be done from the departure list.

A computer-generated departure screen is shown in Fig. 5.15 (overleaf).

```
┌──────────────────────────────────────────────────────────────────────┐
│ ═                         IGS HOTEL                              ▼ ▲   │
│                    DEPARTURES IN 0 NIGHTS                              │
│    1    TWIN    1 ADULT(S)                                             │
│                   ADULT(S)                                             │
│    2    TWIN    1 ADULT(S)                                             │
│    3    TWIN    1 ADULT(S)                                             │
│    5    TWIN    1 ADULT(S)                                             │
│    6    TWIN      ADULT(S)                                             │
│    9    DBLE    2 ADULT(S)                                             │
│   10    DBLE    1 ADULT(S)                                             │
│                   ADULT(S)                                             │
│   11    DBLE    1 ADULT(S)                                             │
│   15    SNGL    1 ADULT(S)                                             │
│                   ADULT(S)                                             │
│   16    SNGL    1 ADULT(S)                                             │
│   18    SNGL    1 ADULT(S)                                             │
│   19    TWNS      ADULT(S)                                             │
│   21    TWNS      ADULT(S)                                             │
│                   ADULT(S)                                             │
│   40    FP      1 ADULT(S)                                             │
│   41    FP      1 ADULT(S)                                             │
│   47    TWIN    1 ADULT(S)                                             │
│ *=ALLOCATED ROOM   #=PERSON DUE OUT, NOT ENTIRE ROOM                   │
│                              ▓                                         │
│ PRINTER 01 OFF LINE                                      03407CON      │
└──────────────────────────────────────────────────────────────────────┘
```

Fig. 5.15 *Departure screen.*

Function/tour list/10-day forecast

All the previous lists and notifications are prepared daily. Once a week the reception department will distribute a list of functions and tours that are booked for the following 10 days. This list assists in the planning of staffing levels over the period, and ensures that staff are aware of projected levels of occupancy in the week to come.

Call/papers/early morning tea (EMT)

The reception department may keep a sheet at the front desk recording the exact time at which guests wish to be called in the morning, their newspaper order and a request for early morning tea or breakfast (Fig. 5.16). Increasing use is being made of semi-automatic equipment in this area to relieve the pressure on staff during the morning peak. Small hotels will install alarm clocks in guest rooms, along with tea-making equipment. Breakfast order forms are also placed in the room for the guest to complete and hang outside the door at night.

Modern telephone systems will have an automated early call system. Using voice prompts, this will instruct the guest to program in a wake-up time using the telephone buttons. The better systems will pick up the guest's nationality from the front office property management system (PMS) and the instruction will be in their language. This can be particularly useful for Japanese or Russian guests who may have limited language skills.

	Room	Paper	E.M.T.		Room	Paper	E.M.T.		Room	Paper	E.M.T.
7.00				7.45				8.30			
7.15	310	Guardian	1	8.00	207	Times	2	8.45			
7.30	709	Sun	–	8.15				9.00			

Fig. 5.16   *Part of an early call, newspapers and early morning tea sheet.*

Guest history cards

Luxury hotels have always used guest history cards to record details of each individual stay by guests, and information on their personal likes and dislikes. 'Transient' hotels have less need of this, due to the short average stay of the guest, the uniformity of hotel facilities and the fact that the guest is unlikely to make a return visit. The cost of keeping a guest history system up-to-date is thought by many hotels to outweigh the benefits. This can be alleviated by the use of a modified system for regular visitors to the hotel (Fig. 5.17) or by ensuring that guest history is part of a computer reservation program, so that it can be easily analysed for more effective marketing, or used to provide a more personalised service.

Name Sparrow, Mr. George				
Address 11 Field Lane, Warmington Tel. 051 235 1234				
Remarks Likes high room. A/c to Birds Ltd.				
Arrival	Departure	Room	Rate	Bill total
14/5	15/5	723	£20	56 70

Fig. 5.17   *Guest history sheet.*

Departure

As the guest leaves there are a number of tasks that have to be completed by reception. Once the bill has been paid the cashier will either pass the registration card back to reception, or send a notification. The receptionist should then remove the guest name from the room status system and mark the room as 'vacant but not ready'.

Notification of the departure should be made to the relevant departments (housekeeping, porters and switchboard) so that they may update their house lists. The housekeeper will then be able to assign a maid to clean a room, and when it has been inspected the room will be returned to reception and it will be possible to re-let the accommodation. Extra departures and extensions of stay are notified to departments separately to ensure that they are not overlooked.

Summary

The flow chart in Fig. 5.18 shows the tasks that the receptionist carries out while the guest is staying in the hotel. The aim of the reception department should be to see that all the tasks are carried out quickly and efficiently, without the guest being aware of the organisation that is needed to make their stay a pleasurable one.

Assignment

Design a registration card suitable for a 'lodge' hotel at a motorway junction. It should include your country's legal requirements.

RECEPTION TASKS **GUEST ACTION**

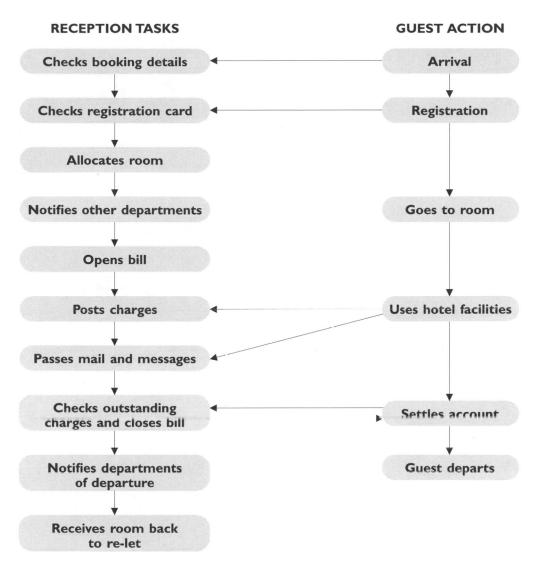

Fig. 5.18 *Flowchart of guest stay.*

CHAPTER 6

Guest Accounting

After studying this chapter you should be able to

- identify the principles of guest billing
- examine the methods of preparing guest bills
- explain the basis of accounting systems
- outline the additional tasks of bill office staff

Principles of hotel billing

Every hotel needs to record the income it receives for selling its goods and services. At the simplest level this will be a cash register in each department and a central cash book showing all the income. Most hotels, however, allow guests to charge purchases to their account and pay the total on departure. Any system of recording charges should satisfy the following requirements:

- Guest bills should be kept up to date.
- Sales of different departments should be identifiable.
- Balancing should be possible.
- Control checks can be carried out.
- It should be easy to operate.
- It should be economical in time and money.

Guest bills should be kept up to date

Because hotels operate throughout 24 hours, guests may incur charges at any time of the day or night, and it should be possible for them to know what their total bill is at any time. Posting to bills should be carried out regularly throughout the day. It is essential that charges are quickly transferred from the sales points in the hotel to the bill office or some charges may be lost to the establishment. The smallest hotels may have to rely upon staff to take charge vouchers by hand, while some hotels were built with a pneumatic tube system sending vouchers from the point of sale to the bill office by metal carriers.

By far the quickest and most efficient system is to install a computer terminal at each point of sale so that information can be transferred directly to the main computer in the bill office.

The busiest time of day in the bill and cash office is the morning, when guests are checking out. It is vital that charges are transferred and posted quickly during this period so that they are charged to guests before they depart. Hotels that charge separately for breakfast must have very efficient methods to post charges at this time or revenue may be lost. For this reason, some hotels include breakfast charges with the apartment rate, which is charged in advance.

Sales of different departments should be identifiable

The charges incurred must be identifiable to the guest, and also to the hotel. If the tariff is inclusive, then there will only be a daily charge on the guest's bill, but the hotel will require some breakdown of charges for control purposes.

The standard system of hotel accounting allows for the identification of sales and cost centres. Even the smallest hotel will wish to have a system of billing that can identify the spending of guests on lunch and dinner, and possibly they will wish to divide it further into the amounts spent on food and drink during these meals.

In many smaller hotels it is the function of the front office staff to perform the duties of restaurant cashiering, although the sophistication of the operation in the larger establishments has ensured that it is a specialised task. Most systems will provide at least a duplicate bill, with a clear final total, and allow for some system of analysis regarding the final method of payment and the volume of the business done.

In setting up the system of billing it is important to provide enough information for the management, without producing so much that nothing at all can be done with it.

Balancing is possible

Wherever cash or charges are recorded it is essential that a balance can be derived. The total of charges incurred should always match the accounts outstanding or the bills paid. This balancing should be made a simple operation so that a quick guide to the accuracy of the posting is obtained.

Control checks can be carried out

Built into all hotel billing systems should be a method of checking that all transactions are being carried out and recorded. The system should be arranged so that cash sales to 'chance' guests are recorded and separated from the 'charged' business. All cash should be recorded separately and the totals independently verified. A check should be made to see that all charges are being correctly posted, and finally there is no dishonest use of the hotel's facilities by customers or staff.

It should be easy to operate

The most effective hotel billing systems are those that record the individual entry the smallest number of times, and where certain procedures are carried out automatically. A complex system such as the tabular ledger will often result in a greater number of errors and omissions, to the detriment of the hotel and the discomfort of the guest. With the most modern computer systems the charge has only to be entered once, and it is automatically entered directly onto the bill.

It should be economical in both time and money

The system installed must not only be economical to operate, but also economical to install. This will depend not only upon the size of the hotel, but also the tariff structure and the volume of individual transactions. A resort hotel with an inclusive daily or weekly charge can operate with a less sophisticated billing system than a 'transient' hotel of half the size. In installing a billing system a full analysis should be undertaken to establish the needs of the hotel. Part of the analysis should cover the availability of staff to operate the installed system, and the amount of management time needed to carry out control checks.

Type of system

The decision regarding the type of accounting system will rest upon a number of things, and it is by no means confined only to the size of the operation.

The Lindrick Hotel, a 23-bedroom privately owned hotel on the outskirts of Sheffield, chooses a tabular ledger, believing it is more in keeping with their old building and the service which they offer to their traditional clientele. The 'tab' is entered on a daily basis (Fig. 6.1, overleaf).

The lack of a preprinted or a pre-produced format means that a tabular ledger has maximum flexibility, and if the nature of the business should change, a hotel can respond at once by changing the headings on the tab. From the information posted to the tabular ledger, a monthly summary is produced for management statistics (Fig. 6.2, page 115). Like that of the tab, the format of the monthly summary could easily be changed to adapt to changed needs.

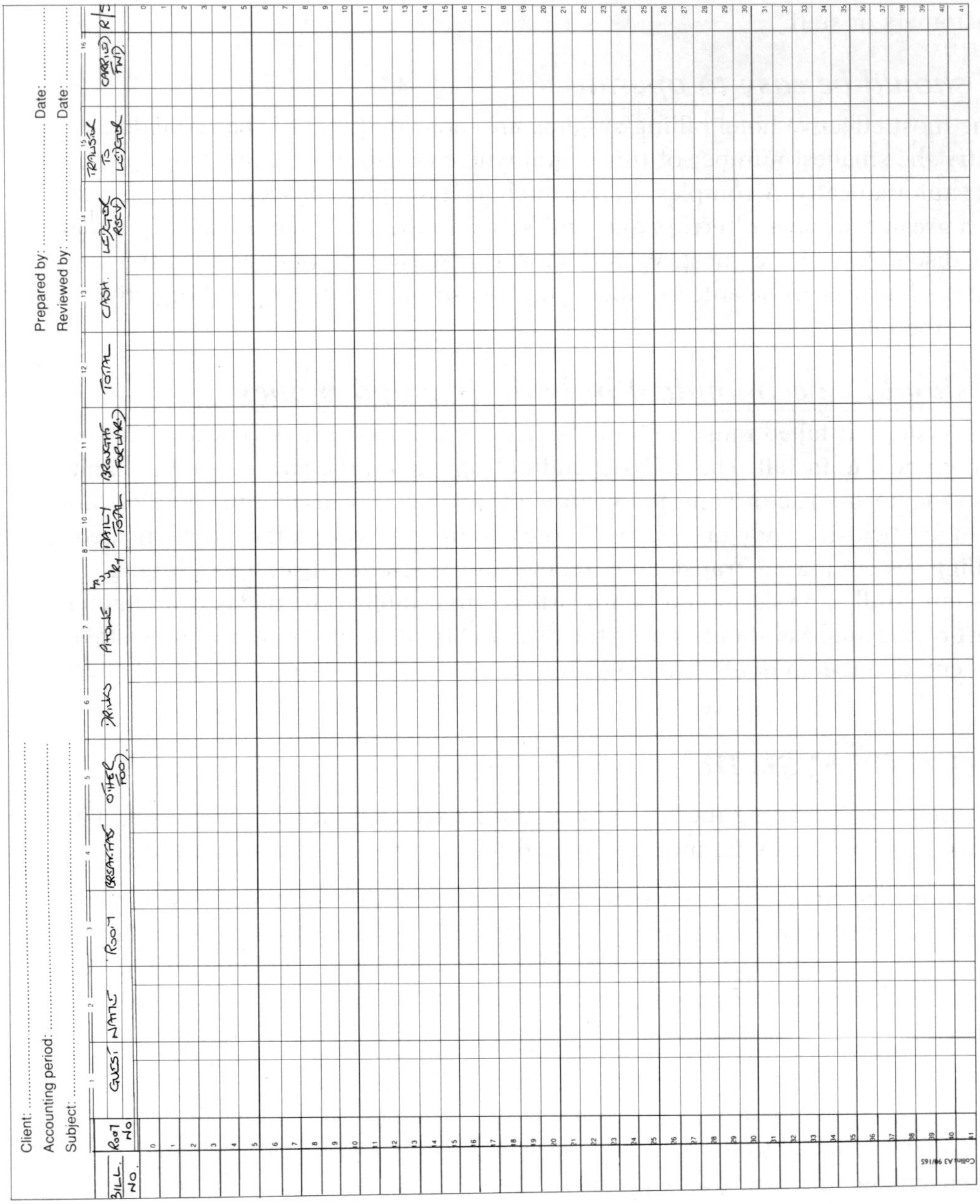

Client: ....

Accounting period: ....

Subject: ....

Prepared by: .... Date: ....

Reviewed by: .... Date: ....

BILL NO	ROOT NO	GUEST NAMES	ROOT	BREAKFAST	OTHER FOOD	DRINKS	APOLLE	PHONE	DAILY TOTAL	BROUGHT FORWARD	TOTAL	CASH	LEDGER POSTG	TRANSFER TO LEDGER	CARRIED FWD	R/S
	1	2		4	5	6	7	8	10	11	12	13	14	15	16	

Fig. 6.1 A tabular ledger.

MONTHLY SUMMARY APRIL 1997

DATE	ROOM	B'FAST	OTHER FOOD	DRINK	PHONE	LAUNDRY	SUB-TOTAL	NEWS	ROOM EXEMPT	VAT PHONE	C'BOX	SUB-TOTAL	DAILY TOTAL	BROUGHT FORWARD	TOTAL	CASH RECEIVED	LEDGER RECEIVED	TRANSFER TO LEDGER	CARRIED FORWARD	OCC R	OCC S
1	273.90	36.00	24.40	6.55			340.85	1.80	39.60			41.40	382.25	224.45	606.70	90.50			516.20	10	13
2	489.90	57.00		12.65			559.55	3.53	39.60			43.13	602.68	516.20	1118.88	548.88			570.00	17	20
3	361.90	42.00	23.00	64.00	14.76		505.66	3.28	39.60			42.88	548.54	570.00	1118.54	244.48		146.26	727.80	13	15
4	202.20	30.00			2.34		234.54	0.90	20.80			21.70	256.24	727.80	984.04	147.00		134.84	702.20	7	10
5	535.20	87.00			0.72		622.92	1.75	20.80			22.55	645.47	702.20	1347.67	878.41	415.69		884.95	22	29
6	397.20	69.00					466.20	0.75	20.80			21.55	487.75	884.95	1372.70	615.66	75.66		832.70	18	20
7	435.90	48.00	36.85	69.45	19.82		610.02	2.08	39.60			41.68	651.70	832.70	1484.40	553.27		45.95	885.18	14	17
8	353.90	36.00	22.65	66.40	3.60		482.55	1.73	39.60			41.33	523.88	885.18	1409.06	266.01	10.00		1153.05	14	16
9	577.90	66.00	76.90	66.70	0.18		787.68	1.45	39.60			41.05	828.73	1153.05	1981.78	906.08			1075.70	22	26
10	559.90	69.00	60.60	85.45	28.18		803.13	1.10	39.60			40.70	843.83	1075.70	1919.53	1436.84	82.00	637.59	-72.90	22	27
11	583.20	87.00		76.50			746.70	1.45	20.80			22.25	768.95	-72.90	696.05	673.60	40.00		62.45	23	30
12	622.20	93.00			16.92		732.12	3.25	20.80			24.05	756.17	62.45	818.62	687.62			131.00	24	32
13	287.20	36.00					323.20	0.50	20.80			21.30	344.50	131.00	475.50	59.00			416.50	12	13
14	561.20	81.00	77.60	7.05	1.80		728.65	1.90	20.80			22.70	751.35	416.50	1167.85	258.35		41.55	867.95	23	27
15	525.90	78.00	67.95	6.90	3.42		682.17	2.30	39.60			41.90	724.07	867.95	1592.02	352.37			1239.65	23	27
16	536.90	78.00	63.80	10.75			689.45	2.23	39.60			41.83	731.28	1239.65	1970.93	834.53	50.00		1086.40	23	27
17	588.90	75.00	59.05	239.77	16.38		979.10	3.29	39.60			42.89	1021.99	1086.40	2108.39	1606.21	87.90	76.20	513.88	20	26
18	496.20	63.00	5.00				564.20	1.48	20.80			22.28	586.48	513.88	1100.36	108.56		366.00	625.80	20	21
19	682.20	90.00			2.70		774.90	1.70	20.80			22.50	797.40	625.80	1423.20	659.95			763.25	23	29
20	381.20	48.00			0.36		429.56	1.35	20.80			22.15	451.71	763.25	1214.96	108.71			1106.25	15	16
21	587.90	81.00	33.95	3.50			706.35	1.75	39.60			41.35	747.70	1106.25	1853.95	358.35		171.00	1324.60	23	28
22	601.90	87.00	52.40	206.05	4.68		952.03	1.95	39.60			41.55	993.58	1324.60	2318.18	626.31	255.83		1947.70	23	30
23	544.90	78.00	35.50	8.75	6.66		673.81	1.38	39.60			40.98	714.79	1947.70	2662.49	342.95		77.96	2241.58	22	28
24	697.20	96.00	28.50	100.00			921.70	2.93	20.80			23.73	945.43	2241.58	3187.01	788.80		563.66	1834.55	23	29
25	705.20	87.00		130.00			922.20	4.05	20.80			24.85	947.05	1834.55	2781.60	862.60			1919.00	23	29
26	755.00	90.00			8.64		853.64	4.70				4.70	858.34	1919.00	2777.34	419.14	34.00	380.00	2012.20	24	30
27	375.00	45.00				3.78	423.78	0.45				0.45	424.23	2012.20	2436.43	313.78			2122.65	14	16
28	630.70	72.00	31.40	100.00			834.10	3.95	18.80			22.75	856.85	2122.65	2979.50	458.60			2520.90	22	25
29	672.70	81.00	35.10	94.15	12.42		895.37	3.05	18.80			21.85	917.22	2520.90	3438.12	607.62		42.35	2788.15	23	28
30	677.70	78.00	15.20	5.30	7.02		783.22	3.15	18.80			21.95	805.17	2788.15	3593.32	996.47	340.00		2936.85	22	28
31														2936.85							
TOTAL	15701.20	2064.00	749.85	1359.92	150.60	3.78	20029.35	65.18	820.80	0.00		885.98	20915.33	35960.64	53939.12	16810.65	1341.08	2733.36	35736.19	587	712
VAT	2339.97	307.60	111.75	202.67	22.44	0.56	2985.00					885.98	2985.00								
TOTAL	13361.23	1756.40	638.10	1157.25	128.16	3.22	17044.35					885.98	17930.33								
DOUBLE CHECK LINE							17044.35					885.98	17930.33						35736.19		

Fig. 6.2 Monthly summary produced from daily tab sheets.

115

By contrast, the Castle Hotel in Lincoln has a similar number of bedrooms and is also privately owned, but although they use the same system in principle, they have made maximum use of information technology, without installing a customised system, or using a recognised package which may not suit all their needs. IT is utilised both in advance reservations, where they have a wide range of standard and form letters, but also in accounting, where the principles of a tabular ledger have been transferred to a spreadsheet. The prices are preset for the rooms, allowing the breakdown of the cost of the room into apartment and food and beverage. The formula is entered to make sure this calculation is performed as a matter of course and a wide range of reports and statistics can be produced with the minimum of effort (Fig. 6.3).

Tabular ledger

For many years this method of recording charges in hotels was the only one in existence, and for several years after the introduction of electronic accounting and in the early days of computerisation it continued to be the most common method in use. In its simplest form it is an adaption of the 'sales day book' for hotels. The advantage of using this system is that hotels can head up the columns according to their needs and should they change over a period of time, no extra costs are incurred.

Although still used by many smaller hotels, in many units it has been replaced by computerisation, since computer programs are now available to suit all types and sizes of hotels. Even so, the principle of the 'tab' and its double entry of charges is applicable to all sorts of hotel billing, and students who are familiar with its operation will easily adapt to other, more sophisticated means of accounting.

The system revolves around two records. One is the customer's account, and the other is the tab sheet. The tab sheet is the summary of all the charges incurred by all guests during the day and forms the basis of the hotel's record of earnings. The customer's bill is normally prepared in duplicate, one copy being given to the guest upon departure and the other retained by the hotel for control purposes.

Layout of the tab will take one of two forms, either vertical or horizontal.

Vertical tabular ledger

The room numbers of guests are entered across the tab and the charges are recorded vertically below each room number (Fig. 6.5, page 122). This system is often used in hotels where carbon paper is used to enter charges onto both the tab and the bill at the same time. Debit entries form the main body of the tab,

Summary of revenue   the Castle Hotel, Westgate, Lincoln   LN1 3AS

R	Slps	Rate	B/fwd	ACCOM	B/FST	LUNCH	DINNER	SNACKS	HerBAR	WINE	BAR	NEWS	PHONE	MISC	GRATS	BALANCE	CASH	CHEQUE	D/CARDS	C/CARDS	LEDGER	C/fwd	Ref
1	2	85.00	0.00	46.00	6.00		30.00		3.00	4.75	4.20					93.95						93.95	A
1	2	65.00	0.00	59.00	6.00											65.00						65.00	B
1	2	65.00	0.00	59.00	6.00											65.00						65.00	C
1	2	60.00	120.00	54.00	6.00											180.00			180.00 Pd by E			0.00	D
1	2	60.00	194.90	54.00	6.00						6.90		9.20			271.00			271.00 Wi D			0.00	E
1	2	65.00	0.00	59.00	6.00						7.40		0.45			72.85			72.85			0.00	F
1	1	75.00	0.00	69.00	6.00		28.05				3.50					106.55						106.55	G
1	1	62.50	0.00	43.00	3.00		15.00		1.50							62.50						62.50	H
1	2	85.00	0.00	46.00	6.00		30.00		3.00	1.95						86.95						86.95	K
1	3	130.00	0.00	71.50	9.00		45.00		4.50	15.25	1.00					146.25						146.25	L
1	1	32.50	0.00	29.50	3.00			2.70			6.20					41.40				41.40 Wi>T	To T	0.00	M
1	1	55.00	0.00	52.00	3.00											55.00						55.00	N
1	1	55.00	0.00	52.00	3.00								3.00			58.00	58.00					0.00	O
1	1	32.50	0.00	29.50	3.00								0.60			33.10				33.10 Pd by M		0.00	P
1	1	75.00	0.00	69.00	6.00											75.00				75.00		0.00	R
1	1	55.00	0.00	52.00	3.00											55.00						55.00	S
1	1	45.00	0.00	42.00	3.00											45.00				45.00 Pd by M		0.00	T
1	1	45.00	0.00	0.00	0.00											0.00						0.00	U
1	1	55.00	0.00	52.00	3.00								6.80			61.80		61.80 d				0.00	W
1							37.85				8.60					46.45	20.00		27.40			0.00	
29			314.90	938.50	87.00	0.00	185.90	2.70	12.00	21.95	37.80	0.00	20.05	0.00	0.00	1620.80	78.00	61.80	551.25	194.50	0.00	735.25	TOTALS

Reference carry-forward summary:

Ref	C/fwd
A	93.95
B	65.00
C	65.00
D	0.00
E	0.00
F	0.00
G	106.55
H	62.50
K	86.95
L	146.25
M	0.00
N	55.00
O	0.00
P	0.00
R	0.00
S	55.00
T	0.00
U	0.00
W	0.00
1	0.00
2	0.00
3	0.00
4	0.00
5	0.00
6	0.00
?	-0.95
£	0.00
TOTAL Pd	735.25

LEDGER a/c's PAID 0.00
BANKING FIGURES
TOTAL CASH+CHEQUES TO BANK   139.80 PDQ   745.75

LEDGER PAYMENTS
£	Details/name in wh'ompayment made
0.00	Total ledger payments 2day

NOTES:
ol Two cheques, £30.00 & £31.80

OCCUPANCY STATISTICS AND SUMMARY OF DAILY TAKINGS

ACCOMMODATION STATISTICS
Rooms available	0
Rooms let	18
Beds available	33
No of sleepers	29

FOOD STATISTICS
Total lunches served	0
Total dinners served	13
No of chance dinner served	3

Average room rate	52.14
Average sleeper rate	32.36
Room occupancy %	ERR
Sleeper occupancy %	87.88
Average spend (lunch)	0.00
Average spend (dinner)	14.30
Resident diner %	34.48

SALES	VAT inc	VAT	VAT ex
Accommodation	938.50	139.78	798.72
Food	275.60	41.05	234.55
Liquor	71.75	10.69	51.06
Newspapers	0.00	0.00	0.00
Telephones	20.05	2.99	17.06
Sundries	0.00	0.00	0.00
Gratuities	0.00	0.00	0.00
TOTAL SALES	1305.90	194.50	1111.40

Signature ....

Date ..../........./1997

Fig. 6.3   Spreadsheet adapted from a tab ledger.

while the credits are entered at the bottom, after the daily total has been summarised.

Each day's tab would consist of a number of similar sheets. The exact number of sheets used would depend upon the number of rooms let.

Horizontal tabular ledger

With the horizontal tab, the departmental charges are listed across the tab, so each guest's account is arranged horizontally across the page of the tab (Fig. 6.4). Debit charges to the guest's account are entered on the left-hand side and credit entries on the right. Normally, two lines are allowed for each room number. This enables a number of entries to be made under the departmental heading; for example, a guest may have a number of telephone calls in the course of a day.

Opening bills

Few tabs are printed with the room numbers on, because occupancy generally varies too much from one period to the next. A new account is opened by heading the bill with the following:

- name of the guest
- rate
- date of arrival
- number of sleepers
- room number

At the same time, an entry is made on the tab showing the same information.

The tab is in room number order at the start of each day, but as departures occur and new guests arrive, this sequence is very quickly spoilt. When a new guest checks in, a tab entry must be made for them. The only place it can be made is at the end of the tab sheet. If in a 50-room hotel there are ten arrivals during the day, then these ten arrivals will have to be entered onto the end of the sheet. The entries will be in the order the guests arrive, not numerically in order of the rooms. For example, the guests for Room 38 may arrive before those for Room 7. For this reason much of the time of the bill office clerks may be spent searching through the tab sheets to locate room numbers, so that they may enter charges onto the guest account.

Posting charges

Room charges for new guests are normally entered as they arrive, and all other room charges are entered at a set time of day (e.g. 1800 hours) Other charges are entered from charge vouchers as they arrive in the bill office. The most effective method is to post the charge onto the guest's bill, and then onto the tab sheet, and finally to cross through the charge voucher to show that it has been dealt with. If a sequence such as this is always followed, then it is unlikely

TABULAR DAILY REPORT & CONTROL OF BUSINESS DONE

DAY OF WEEK .... TUESDAY

DATE .... 23 JUNE

Inv. Number	Guest's Name	Room No.	Sleepers	Room	Breakfast	Food	Dinner	Bar	Wines	Telephone	Other	Daily Total	Balance B/F from Previous day	Grand Total	Cash Received	Ledger Received	Accounts Transferred to Ledger	Carried Forward
10975	GREEN MR/S	101	2	40 00	5 00		15 80	7 90	9 20			77 90	56 00	133 90				133 90
10976	BROWN MR.J	102	1	25 00	2 50	4 90		2 40				34 80	35 00	69 80				69 80
10977	JAUNE MR.Y	104	1	25 60	1 75					8 20		34 95	102 00	136 95		4 20		132 75
10978	PINK MS L	106	1		2 50					40		2 90	48 90	51 80	51 80			-
10979	BLACK MR&b	103	2	40 00	5 00							45 00		45 00				45 00

Fig. 6.4 Horizontal tabular ledger.

that any stage will be left out. Also, the bill is always up to date, so guests will always be charged for items they have consumed.

Allowances

If a charge is incorrectly entered, then an allowance will have to be made. This is done on the credit section of the tab, and is shown as a deduction on the guest's bill. For example, a breakfast charge of £3.50 may be incorrectly charged to Room 38 instead of Room 83. An entry will also be made in the allowance book, which is checked daily by the management. The allowance book explains the reason for each allowance, and acts as a quick control check.

Departures

As a guest checks out, their bill is totalled and the top copy presented to them for payment. The method of payment is noted on the bill, and the bill is receipted. The tab is then totalled to agree with the bill, and the payment entered in the appropriate column on the credit part of the tab. A pencil line is then drawn through the guest's name and room number. This serves two purposes. Firstly, it shows that the guest has checked out, and secondly, it ensures that no charges for an incoming guest are inadvertently posted into the wrong account.

Room changes

If a guest changes room during their stay, then the new number has to be noted on both the bill and the tab. This is done by crossing the old room number through and writing the new room number above it. When this happens the bill office clerk has to make sure that checks from departments are posted to the correct room number. It is also important at this stage to check to see if there is a change to the room rate, and if so this must be recorded.

Cash sales

Cash sales from the restaurant and bars will be recorded on the tab ledger, along with the rest of the day's business. In this way the tab is a complete record of the hotel's trading for a 24-hour period.

Balancing

The exact time of closing the tab will depend upon the staffing in the office, and the work pattern of the hotel. Balancing may be carried out either at 1500 hours or at the end of the evening shift.

The ability to 'balance' the accounts at the end of a day's trading is the basis of all double-entry book-keeping. The balance ensures that both sides of the account are equal.

The major balancing features are as follows:

- the debit side will equal the credit side;
- cash taken should equal the cash column of the tab;
- the credit column should equal transfers to the ledger;
- the carried forward column will be equal to the total of outstanding bills.

A hotel may also wish to make other checks, relating to the various departments, and the total amount that each department has sold. Despite the checks that a balance allows, some errors will not be located through the balancing process. Such errors might include

- errors of omission   • errors of commission   • compensating errors

The tab that is reproduced in Fig. 6.5 will balance *but*

1   Calculate the total of all the guests' bills: the residents owe £778.75
2   Add together the amounts taken by each department: also £778.75
3   Room 102 owes £255.78 but a dinner bill has been left off for £25.50
4   Room 102 was overcharged yesterday for a telephone call (£4.40); should have been charged to Room 103
5   Check the addition for Room 101
6   Check the addition for the telephone department

Points 1 and 2 are the first balance – this is the stage that most staff are grateful to reach.

Point 3 represents an **error of omission**. In this case it does not affect the balance at all, but it is a serious mistake because it will cost the hotel money

Point 4 represents an example of an **error of commission**. This is where the charge is posted to the wrong bill or the wrong department. It may not be noticed for some time, since the balance is not affected, and in this case it is not too serious, because the second client is still in residence, but clearly potentially such errors can affect the final figures quite seriously.

Points 5 and 6 represent a **compensating error**: although Room 101 has been overcharged by £0.30, the telephone column has been added incorrectly, and is in fact also £0.30 overcast. The tab will still balance, but neither account is correct.

Some hotels that operate a tab ledger produce two guest bills. One is a three-day bill for short-stay guests, and the other is an eight-day bill for guests who stay for a longer time. The bills are exactly the same, apart from the greater number of columns on the eight-day bill. In principle, the most common bill is calculated on a five-day period, since this reflects the main volume of business in most hotels (Fig. 6.6, page 123).

12 JUNE

SLEEPERS

	101		102		103		104											DAILY TOTAL	
ROOM NO.	101		102		103		104												
NAME	Jarrold Mr.&MrsT.		Spain Miss B.		Slaney Mrs. C.		Ray. Mr.&Mrs												
RATE	R.O. £90 (2		R+B £60 (1		R+B. £60 (1		R.O. £90 (2												
B/F	101	90	181	18	68	12												351	20
APARTMENTS	90	00	55	00	55	00	90	00										290	00
PENSION																		—	—
BREAKFASTS	12	00	5	00	5	00												22	00
LUNCHEONS					4	80												4	80
TEAS			4	20														4	20
DINNERS	42	90																42	90
EARLY TEAS																		—	—
BEVERAGES	2	00			1	40												3	40
WINES	12	90			2	80												15	70
SPIRITS & LIQUEURS	14	40																14	40
BEERS																			
MINERALS	1	75																1	75
TELEPHONES	8	30			v/c 11/6 4	40												13	00
V.P.O'S			8	60			5	00										13	60
NEWSPAPERS			1	80														1	80
TOTAL	286	45	255	78	141	52	95	00										778	75
CASH			200	00														200	00
ALLOWANCES			o/c TEL 4	40														4	40
LEDGER																		—	
BALANCE C/F	286	45	51	38	141	52	95	00										574	35

Fig. 6.5 Completed tabular ledger.

INVOICE No. **27970**

ROOM No. ....

....

....

....

VAT No. 391 1884 32

Philip C Taylor M.H.C.I.M.A., Master Innholder.

Lindrick Hotel
226 Chippinghouse Road,
Sheffield. S7 1DR.

Telephone: (0114) 258 5041
Fax: (0114) 255 4758

Date							
Accommodation & Breakfast							
Dinner							
Teas/Coffees							
Other Foods							
Bar Drinks							
Wines							
Newspapers							
Telephone							
Daily Total							
Brought Forward							
Carried Forward							

Fig. 6.6 *A standard guest bill.*

Machine billing

Using machines for hotel billing is essentially the same as the tabular ledger. All the machine does is carry out the tasks of the bill office automatically, as charges are being posted. The principle of double-entry book-keeping is exactly the same.

A hotel billing machine should be thought of as two machines in one. The first acts as an adding machine and posts charges onto guests' bills and notes the new balance. The second keeps a cumulative total of the amount charged to each department.

The number of hotels using these machines is now very small, since replacement parts for the machines are hard to obtain, and a simple personalised computer package can be obtained for the same cost.

Computer billing

Many people erroneously believe that only large hotels will benefit from the use of a computer, but billing this way can be cost-effective even for the smallest hotel. Many systems can be linked to other areas such as the switchboard, and for some hotels the computer system has expanded to ensure that staff no longer waste time doing boring work but have more time to spend looking after the guests.

Benefits of computer billing

The main benefit associated with billing of this type is that programs can be personalised, so that each hotel can review its needs and install a system based upon them. There are many hundreds of systems available, some able to perform virtually every task that will be required in the hotel. It is at this point that it is important to be selective, since it is of no use to an establishment to buy a system which it will never use to the full. Many hotels feel secure in using a system that is tried and tested, and familiar through use in some of the major companies, but the choice is virtually limitless, and will be made on the basis of personal preference and need.

Operating a computer

The operation of the computer will vary according to the system; they follow no standard pattern. Nevertheless it is possible to make one or two generalisations:

• Room charges will be processed automatically.
• VAT will be calculated at the appropriate rate, excluding items that are zero-rated.

- A wrong charge will not be accepted onto a bill if the error is user-induced.
- A variety of reports will be compiled as charges are made.

Opening a bill

If the reservation is an advanced booking, guest details will already be stored under the booking reference number but the room number can be added effortlessly and the information amended if necessary. Advance deposits that have already been recorded will be transferred to the account after check-in.

Posting charges

If the system includes terminals at points of sale, a great deal of time is saved posting charges. The information can be entered directly in the sales areas and the bill office clerk is saved the monotony of sorting and posting vouchers. Many of the charges (e.g. wine, sauna, apartments) are pre-coded, but the codes used to analyse the transactions are identifiable (Fig. 6.7, overleaf).

Adjustments/corrections

Entries to alter previous postings can be made easily, and should it be necessary to move a guest to another room all the existing data will be transferred to the new room.

Closing an account

Once the guest has agreed the total, the computer can be advised how payment is to be made – either in cash or transferred to an account. If the guest has previously indicated that all, or part, of the bill is to be transferred elsewhere, this can be carried out automatically and quickly. In some systems the computer will be programmed only to accept certain charges on main accounts, all else being transferred to extra bills. Most systems are equipped with a foreign exchange calculation facility, thereby eliminating any possible errors when accepting foreign currency in payment of an account.

Balancing

Balancing as such does not really exist with a computer, since so many possible errors have been eliminated at source.

Information is readily available and the audit trail can be displayed at any time. The-end-of-the-day routine is quick and easy, and in some establishments is little more than an automatic accounting record for the day's business. However, a selection of reports and information (i.e. room sales, projected sleeper occupancy) are readily available to management, providing them with the vital up-to-the-minute information essential for effective forward planning.

Garden Court®

NOTTINGHAM

Castle Marina Park, Nottingham, NG7 1GX
Telephone: (0115) 993 5000
Fax: (0115) 993 4000

```
Pg.  1        17AUG 97      21AUG 97

Room: 231 STATEMENT




17AUG       231 Accommodation & Breakfast
18AUG       231 Accommodation & Breakfast        55.00
            1842 Phone-Auto                      55.00
            2041 Bar Dinner                       3.00
19AUG       231 Accommodation & Breakfast         4.00
            2037 Phone-Auto                      55.00
            2158 Late Bar                          .75
            2158 Late Bar Fd                       .95
20AUG       231 Accommodation & Breakfast         8.85
             20 Phone-Auto                       55.00
            2259 Bar Dinner                       4.75
            2259 Rest Dinner                       .95
21AUG       231 Accommodation & Breakfast        15.20
                                                 55.00

                     *** Total ***              313.45
```

Fig. 6.7   *A computerised guest bill.*

Many hotels produce an end-of-day, or end-of-shift audit pack, containing a variety of information such as

- copies of guest bills   • call sheets   • house lists
- audit reports   • telephone printouts

This control pack is kept for audit purposes for a number of years, and will be referred to in case of queries.

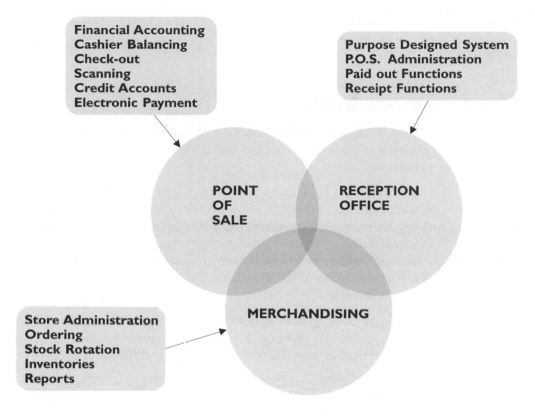

Fig. 6.8 PMS is an essential aid to communication.

Property management systems

Many hotels now see a property management system (PMS) as an essential part of their communications and accounting process (Fig. 6.8). Most systems will incorporate, at the very least, the following:

- reservations
- registration
- guest billing
- check-out

- night audit
- group bookings
- F & B management
- point-of-sale information

- debtors
- creditors
- general ledger

In addition, many systems are linked to the building management system, or other communication systems within the hotel, in order to provide the guest with the 'seamless' service to which they have become accustomed. Most PMSs are now compatible with a range of additional facilities and can interface with other communication systems. Checking in and out can be registered immediately, so room status can be updated instantly. Many systems incorporate a facility for bill viewing in the room, so the clients who are leaving can check their bill in advance, and any queries can be dealt with before they check out.

Control procedures

The basis of control is the independent checking of accounts and charges in the hotel. This is important in any business, but particularly so where cash, food and drink are concerned.

The level of control has to be balanced against the cost of finding and rectifying errors. At a certain stage it is cheaper to allow errors to go undetected because the cost of locating them would be prohibitive. Some hotels overcome this by randomly changing the area of strict control so that a close check is made in each area at some stage. Many hotels no longer operate a control office as such, preferring instead to rely upon the increased efficiency of the machinery in use throughout the establishment.

Regardless of the system in operation, a simple check is normally performed to control the apartment income revenue. Room charges are controlled by agreeing three separate figures; any discrepancies must be followed through and checked.

Figure 6.9 shows the apartment control triangle. A, B and C should be prepared independently of each other and A = B = C.

In some establishments a further check may be made on linen used, to ensure that all rooms have been correctly reported.

Night audit

Large hotels make use of night auditors who work between 2300 and 0800 hours to carry out control tasks, post charges and prepare management reports, and balance the hotel's daily trading accounts. In some units the night auditor will also carry out the separate tasks of night manager, receptionist and security officer.

If the hotel has a late-night food and beverage service, and a busy desk, then a night auditor will be very useful for they will be able to carry out posting through the night. In this way guest accounts will be fully up to date in time for morning departures. A night auditor brings forward by eight hours control procedures and checks on posting and balancing. These eight hours may be critical, for an error may be located and the charge re-posted onto a guest's

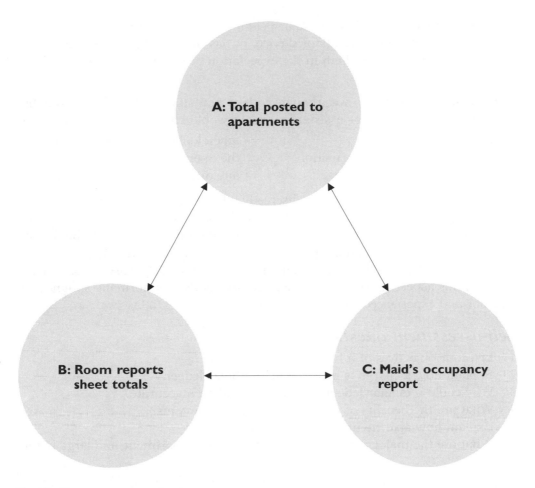

Fig. 6.9 *The apartment control cycle.*

account before departure. Often if a guest leaves before an account is corrected the charge has to be written off as a bad debt.

Potential bad debts

The different pace of work at night and the absence of interruption allows the night auditor to check through current accounts in the bill tray in order to try to identify guests who may be potential bad debts. The first method is to list all bills over a certain figure for the attention of the head cashier. The head cashier is then able to check the booking details to establish the status of the guest. Certainly a chance guest would be a greater credit risk than a guest with a confirmed booking. A second method of checking potential 'walk-outs' is to check the individual bills for unusual spending patterns. A guest who orders large amounts of liquor from floor service, or has high food and beverage charges, may be ordering them in the expectation of not paying the bill at the end of the end of their stay.

In the case of a guest who was thought to be a potential 'walk-out' or 'bad debt', the hotel security officer or assistant manager would check up on the following:

- details of booking
- registration card and information
- contents of room and luggage
- any telephone calls placed through the operator
- any unusual orders for food/drink

All of these checks are carried out discreetly, often without the guest knowing they are going on. The check on luggage would be done when the guest was out of the hotel. If the checks were not satisfactory, then the room would be double locked, or a new key would be issued with a different code, and the guest contacted and asked to bring their bill up to date. Obviously, care needs to be taken in this aspect of control work and consequently it is normally assigned to a senior and experienced member of staff.

Self-assessment questions

1. List four objectives of a hotel billing system.
2. Explain how a charge is posted onto a tabular ledger.
3. Why could a tabular ledger balance, but still be inaccurate?
4. What are the benefits of computer accounting systems?
5. Explain how apartment income is controlled.
6. What are the major advantages of a night audit department in a large hotel?

Assignment

Mr and Mrs J. Wells arrive at the Lindrick Hotel at 0800 hours on 23rd June having flown in from their recent holiday. They had booked in advance, and had been told that a room might not be ready on their arrival. They are allocated Room 18, and are paying £80.00 for the room for the night, inclusive of £7.50 each for breakfast. As the room is not ready they have breakfast, and then leave their luggage and go out. When they return they have a bar snack each, totalling £9.50 with drinks of £4.50. Having paid a cash deposit of £100.00, they go to their room, where they make a telephone call which is charged at £3.80.

They stay for four nights, and have the same bar snack and drinks on the last day as they had on the first. They have a newspaper (£0.45) each day, and dinner on the night of the 25th June (£12.50 each plus £11.75 for wine and

£1.80 for coffee). On the night of the 25th June they go to the theatre, the hotel having purchased tickets on their behalf at their request (total cost £32.00).

Tasks

1   Using the bill for the Lindrick Hotel printed earlier in this chapter, enter the charges for Mr and Mrs Wells.
2   Explain the effect of the cash deposit on the total calculation of the bill.
3   Show how the telephone call could be amended if it was found to be incorrect.
4   Record the total of the bill, and then show how VAT would be extracted. Record the resulting total.

CHAPTER 7

Methods of Payment

After studying this chapter you should be able to

- identify the characteristics of the various methods of payment
- explain how income is banked
- state how elementary control procedures are established

Over the last decade the forms of payment accepted in hotels have changed quite dramatically. Most hotels still accept a variety of methods of payment, mainly for two reasons:

- to provide a service to their clients;
- to generate additional earnings through exchange.

The large majority of independent travellers now use some form of credit or charge card, and hotels have become very familiar with a wide range of cards, often with 'dual' ownership (e.g. the HCIMA have their own version of Barclaycard). Regardless of the method of payment of the majority of main accounts, there will always be a number of other transactions within the hotel, and these will often be paid through a number of other methods.

Cash floats

Every hotel will need a store or 'float' of money to enable it to provide service to the customers, to give change for bills, to allow the bars and other sales areas to operate, and to carry out foreign exchange transactions (within policy limits).

Size of floats

The number of floats in a hotel will vary according to the number of sales outlets. A very small hotel may have just one float, whilst a large hotel with many restaurants may have ten or more separate floats, one for each sales point. The amount of money needed in the float will be a reflection of two things: firstly, the prices charged in departments; and secondly, the number of transactions that are carried out. The higher the number of separate transactions, the greater the size of the float. Another factor that has to be considered is the method of payment used. A hotel that has a large number of foreign guests will need a larger float, for it will not be able to use their foreign currency payments to give change to later customers.

Composition of floats

Individual floats are made up to the agreed amounts in a predetermined way. This composition will again reflect the tariffs of the department concerned. The main cash float of a large hotel will not have a great need for low value coins, for most items will come to round figures. However, this will not be the case in a bar or kiosk. The float is stored in a secure cash drawer in the same way in every department; this enables cashiers to relieve each other, and to transfer from one department to another with the minimum of interference to the process of giving change rapidly and accurately. The layout of the coins in the cash drawer is organised so that a contrast is made between coins that lie next to each other. For example, 50p pieces could be placed next to 5p pieces so that the cashier will not confuse the two by texture, size or weight.

Security

Cash floats are signed for as they are issued, and signed back in again at the end of the day. If there is a handover from one shift to another, then the total amount in the cash drawer is counted and agreed, and the float is passed on to the incoming cashier. Floats are occasionally subjected to spot checks by auditors to ensure that they are correct and no irregularities are occurring. Particularly dangerous would be personal IOUs in floats from individual cashiers. This is forbidden as it reduces the actual cash available to the business and aids the cashier in certain frauds and thefts.

Cost of money

The aim of the hotel should be to keep the lowest number of floats and the amount of money in them to the lowest level possible, while still allowing the business to run smoothly. The first reason for this is the risk of theft or robbery. A large amount of money will be more attractive to a thief. In the event of a robbery, a small float will minimise the loss.

A float also costs money to provide. Any money that the hotel has that is not in the bank is not earning interest or reducing the size of the overdraft. For example, if the interest rate is 5% per annum then a £1000 float will cost £50 per year to maintain in the hotel. If the float can be safely reduced to £500, then this will reflect an additional profit for the hotel.

Methods of payment

Upon departure, guests can settle their account in one of a number of different ways:

- cash
- foreign currency
- cheque
- traveller's cheque
- foreign cheque
- debit card
- credit card
- charge card
- ledger payment
- voucher (e.g. travel agent, A & TO).

In dealing with each of these methods of payment, the hotelier must assess the impact of three major factors: liquidity, security and worth.

Liquidity

If a bill is paid in cash, the hotel can immediately use the money to purchase goods itself, or bank the money and earn interest on it. Payment by ledger, however, will take much longer – perhaps as much as two or three months may pass before the money can be re-used in the business (Fig. 7.1).

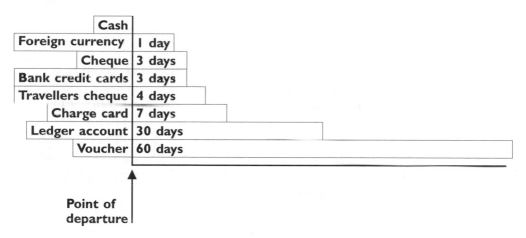

Fig. 7.1 Relative liquidity of various methods of payment

Security

There are two sides to security. The first is the likelihood of forgery or fraud by each of the payment methods; the second is the subsequent risk of theft once the hotel has the money. Payment by cheque is a greater security risk than accepting dollars in payment of the account. However, if the hotel were robbed, it would be difficult to trace stolen currency, whereas cheques would be unlikely to be taken as they would be worthless to a thief.

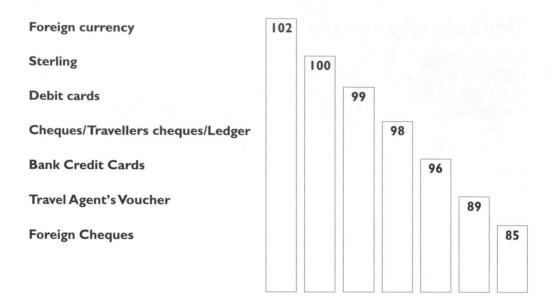

Fig. 7.2 *Amount received in payment of a £100 bill by various methods.*

Worth

Finally, there is the total amount of money the hotel eventually receives in payment. This will not be the same in every case. Handling charges, commission and delays in payment all cost the hotel money. On the other hand, because of the extra commission, accepting payment in foreign currency often means that the hotel gains an extra profit when guests use this method of payment. Figure 7.2 shows the amounts received in payment of a bill for £100. Reference to this index clearly shows that the profitability of the hotel may be affected by the variety of payment methods used by its guests.

Cash

Cash was traditionally the most popular method of paying bills, but as prices have risen and other methods become so readily available it is used much less in hotels where bills for a few days' stay can often amount to hundreds of pounds.

Theoretically, there are upper limits for payment in coin as legal tender, and whilst payment in Scottish pound notes may be accepted, the Channel Islands and Irish currency can only be exchanged at banks. In practice, a hotel would be unlikely to refuse 10 × 50p pieces (legal tender), nor would it insist on payment in legal tender (cash). Nevertheless, all other methods of payment are accepted as a service to customers. Any hotel that insisted upon cash only as a method of settling bills would probably lose a lot of business as a result.

Foreign currency

Tourists and overseas visitors may wish to settle their bill in their own currency. A list of currencies accepted and the exchange rate is kept in the cashier's department. The currencies which are subject to severe exchange rate fluctuations are not accepted. This may be through political instability or because of a lack of trade with the rest of the world. The hotel is not obliged to accept any foreign currency, and many limit themselves to those of the major trading countries of the world. The rate of exchange that the hotel offers is generally less favourable than could be obtained at a bank. This commission covers the cost of providing the service, guards against a sudden change in the exchange rate, and provides the hotel with an extra profit. Coins are not accepted in hotels although some major banks will accept them at around 80% of the current note exchange rate.

In recent years, foreign exchange has become more complex through the 'floating' of sterling against other currencies. This means that the exchange rate will vary over a year, and even from one day to the next. Group hotels overcome this by notifying individual units of the exchange rate to offer. Smaller units can either check with their bank or look in the current daily paper, where major exchange rates are listed. It is a simple matter to add on a fixed percentage to this rate to cover the hotel's costs.

Cashiers have to be trained in the recognition of the major currencies in order to avoid the risk of crude forgeries being passed off as genuine. This also ensures that the cashier will recognise different currencies with the same name, such as American and Canadian dollars.

Cheques

For a while, payment by cheque was one of the most common methods used, and reflected the decline of cash as a method of payment in recent years. This has been aided by the cheque guarantee cards (Fig. 7.3, overleaf). These cards guarantee payment of the cheque up to the agreed amount (usually £50 or £100) provided that a few simple rules are followed.

Cheque guarantee cards guarantee payment provided that

• only one cheque is used per transaction;
• it is signed in the presence of the cashier;
• the bank code on the cheque and the guarantee card agree;
• the card number is written on the reverse side of the cheque;
• the card has not expired.

It is not possible to pay a bill of £100 by issuing two cheques of £50, for the bank does not guarantee to honour this transaction. By putting the card

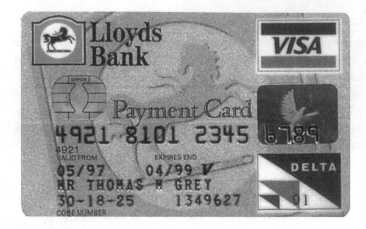

Fig. 7.3   *A cheque guarantee card.*

number on the back of the cheque, the transaction is changed to a cash one, and the customer will not be able to stop the cheque later. It is important that the cashier watches the customer sign the cheque and then compares the signatures carefully to establish that they are similar.

Code number
The bank sorting code number must agree with the code of the issuing cheque.

Card number
The card number is written on the reverse of the cheque by the accepting cashier. It does not correspond to any other number on the cheque.

Expiry date
The card will not be valid if it is out of date.

Signature
The signature must be checked against the signature written on the back of the cheque. The card should be examined to make sure that the signature panel has not been tampered with.

Figure 7.4 shows a typical cheque. Most cheques are now issued crossed and so have to be paid into a bank account. They can be reassigned to a third party by the payee signing the back, but if a third-party cheque is returned, then the hotel has to contact the original drawer of the cheque to obtain settlement. For this reason, hotels do not usually accept third-party cheques.

Date
When accepting a cheque, the cashier should check a number of points, one of the most important being the date. A cheque that has a date in the future on it

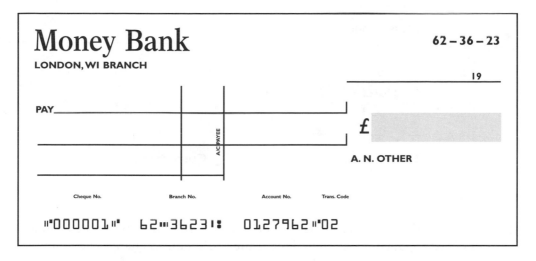

Fig. 7.4 *A personal cheque.*

(a postdated cheque) will not become valid until that date. A cheque more than six months old (stale) is no longer valid.

The most important points to note when accepting a cheque are as follows:

• that the date is correct;
• that the words and figures agree (if they do not, the cheque will not be paid);
• that it is correctly signed, preferably in the sight of the cashier;
• that it is completed in ink rather than in pencil;
• that any alterations are signed (not initialled) by the drawer.

Blank cheques

Blank cheques used to be held by some hotels so that a customer could fill in details of their own bank account number while paying the bill. As the risk of fraud is much greater with cheques of this kind, the banks discourage their use by levying a high service charge on cheques that are paid in by this method. Payment will also take longer as the cheque cannot be electronically sorted and this is now a service which is really only provided by a few luxury hotels.

Crossing cheques

There are a number of rules about crossing cheques. The two most important are as follows:

1   *A/c payee*: this means that the cheque can only be paid into the account of the person nominated. It cannot be assigned to a third party. This is useful for cheques sent by post.

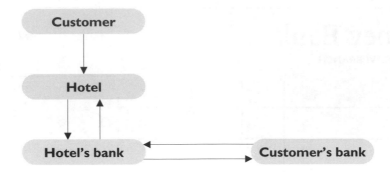

Fig. 7.5 *Special clearance for a cheque during banking hours.*

2   *Not to exceed xxx*: this crossing establishes a maximum value to the cheque and guards against fraud by making it more difficult to change the amount payable.

Cheque authorisation

During banking hours a hotel cashier can quickly establish whether a cheque is good for payment. A telephone call is made to the hotel's bank, with details of the cheque, and the name of the bank and the branch (Fig. 7.5). The bank will contact the manager of the drawer's branch and establish whether the cheque will be passed for payment. The cost of the telephone call for this 'special clearance' is debited to the hotel's account, although some establishments pass it on to the guest. A 'special clearance' is useful when checking out a chance guest whose bill is greater than the cheque card limit. The same procedure is often employed when accepting a company cheque without prior arrangements.

Traveller's cheque

Traveller's cheques (Fig. 7.6) are issued in fixed denominations by major banks, travel agents and now building societies throughout the world. The customer buys them (before leaving home) in their own currency, or in the currency of the country being visited. When they are purchased they have to be signed, and the serial numbers are noted by the issuing bank cashier. Normally a service charge of 1% is paid to the bank by the customer. This covers insurance against loss or theft. If the traveller's cheques are stolen, the issuing company will repay the customer within 24 hours. For this reason, traveller's cheques are much more secure than currency. When accepting payment by traveller's cheque the cashier should watch the guest sign and date the cheque. If there is any doubt about the signature, the customer can be asked to sign again on the reverse of the cheque. This is a very potent weapon against fraud as few people are able to forge a signature without one to copy. Proof of identity can also be verified by

Fig. 7.6   An American Express traveller's cheque.

asking the guest to produce their passport before accepting the traveller's cheque.

Traveller's cheques must then be paid into the bank account of the hotel, normally with the room number of the guest noted on the reverse side so that any queries that arise later can be followed up.

Foreign cheques

Some hotels accept payment by foreign cheques, especially those drawn on banks in Europe which are written in sterling. Since the greater unionisation brought about by the EU, these cheques have largely taken the place of Eurocheques, although it is still possible to obtain both Eurocheques and Eurocheque cards. Before accepting a foreign cheque the cashier will ensure that it is backed by a guarantee card, in the same way that a UK cheque would be. Those hotels which do accept foreign personal cheques often have the rule that they must be approved by a senior member of staff unless the client is a regular one for whom there is an established policy.

Debit cards

Debit cards such as Switch and Delta are now a common alternative to cheques. The outstanding sum is taken directly from the client's account, in the same way that a cheque payment would be, but the transfer is through an electronic point-of-sale system, and no cheque is necessary. Both parties, instead, receive a slip notifying them of the details of the payment. The card used for this purpose is frequently the same card that is used to guarantee a cheque, or withdraw money from a cashpoint (Fig. 7.7, overleaf).

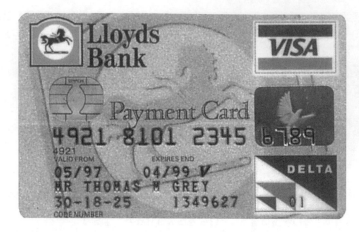

Fig. 7.7   *A cheque guarantee card can also be a debit card.*

Bank credit cards

The two major bank credit cards in the UK are Visa and Access. The cards are issued free to customers and often there is no annual subscription. The customer uses the card to purchase goods and services by signing a sales voucher for the total amount of the bill. At monthly intervals the card company sends a statement to the customer detailing all purchases in the previous month. The customer may pay the total owing, or pay only a proportion of it and pay the rest of it over a period of time. The minimum payment is fixed by the government as the cards constitute a form of credit. When the card is obtained the customer receives a personal credit limit, and that must not be exceeded in any one month.

Visa is an internationally recognised name, and while most countries use an additional name (e.g. Barclaycard in the UK; Carte Bleu in France), all cards carry the name 'Visa' and bear the distinctive blue, white and gold stripe logo (Fig. 7.8).

Access is also international, with world-wide circulation, but it is affiliated to two major cards in other countries and so can be used at establishments displaying signs for Mastercharge or Eurocard. Access cards issued in the UK bear the logo of all three companies.

Charge cards

Charge cards (occasionally called T and E cards) are different in a number of ways. The customer has to pay an annual subscription for the card and has to settle each month's statement in full. There are no facilities for extending repayment. Generally, the credit limit on charge cards will be higher, and

Fig. 7.8 A Barclaycard/Visa card.

they are likely to be used for the purchase of airline tickets, hotel bills and restaurant bills, and also as company charge cards. The procedure for accepting payment by each type of card is broadly the same. The card company offers a franchise to the hotel, which enables the hotel to accept the cards in payment. The hotel is given a 'floor limit' which sets the maximum amount that can be paid by the card without telephoning for authorisation. All major card companies operate a 24-hour authorisation centre where a cashier may make a reverse charge call to check on the validity of a card or obtain clearance to accept payment of a bill above the floor limit. Many front office computer systems also keep a 'stop list' of lost or stolen cards.

Procedure for payment by credit card

1 Check that the bill is inside the 'floor limit'.
2 Obtain the card from the client.
3 Swipe the card through the machine.
4 Ask the client to sign the audit roll (retain the card).
5 Check that the signatures on the card and the voucher agree.
6 Return the card and the top copy to the guest.

In the case of a hotel operating a system that does not have EPOS, it will be necessary to prepare a sales voucher manually, and take an imprint of the client's card on the machine provided. It is useful for all hotels to retain a supply of vouchers and the machine, in case of electric failure, or a breakdown in the EPOS system.

At this point the procedures for dealing with the two card types differ. Charge card sales vouchers are sent to the card company every few weeks, and a cheque is returned in payment, with the commission to the card company subtracted. Bank card sales vouchers are paid into the bank along with cash and cheques, and are credited to the hotel's account in the normal way, again minus a commission charge. The rate of commission will be different between the different card companies, but is commonly between 2% and 5% of the amount billed. The franchise issued by the card companies prohibits the hotel from adding the commission as a surcharge onto the bill of the guest. Because of the different operating systems, bills paid by charge card take longer to settle than bills that are paid by bank credit cards.

Ledger accounts

To encourage customer loyalty, and for convenience, many hotels allow their guests to sign the bill as they depart, and arrange for all charges to be sent to the company or individual at the end of the month for settlement. Ledger payment facilities are only offered after the hotel has established that the customer is creditworthy, either by obtaining satisfactory references from another supplier, or from the customer's bank. Obviously, with a deferred payment there is a greater risk of bad debt, and certainly the hotel will have to wait to get its money, sometimes as much as two or three months after the bill was incurred. When opening a ledger account for a company, the hotel has to obtain a list of authorised users, and agree a limit for individual bills. Some ledger accounts are partial only, the guest being allowed to charge the company for accommodation and meals, but being personally responsible for extras such as laundry and telephone calls. In this case the bill office must run two bills for the guest. Many large hotels or chains operate their own in-house credit card scheme, and this is obviously preferable for the hotel, since they need pay no commission. Many hotels feel that the existence of ledger accounts encourages the users to choose their hotel more frequently, and to spend a greater amount of money.

Vouchers

Travel agents issue vouchers to customers to enable them to settle their hotel bills. This is simply an extension of the ledger system, and the hotel has to take simple precautions to ensure that the agent is respectable. The voucher is normally for specified services and one copy is sent to the hotel with the booking, and the top copy obtained from the client on arrival. All the vouchers from a particular agent are returned, usually at the end of the month, for payment, and when the agent pays the bill they will usually subtract their commission on the accommodation and breakfast charges.

Developments

Bank payment cards currently account for a major proportion of payments, with the associated increase in the amount of fraud. The banks are well aware of the potential problems to organisations and are working towards the introduction of chip technology on all cards, which is a far more secure system than the magnetic stripe. Chip cards, also known as ICC (Integrated Circuit Cards) or SMART cards, represent a significant improvement in security, and will also assist in the processing of more information, resulting in the provision of an increased range of services, such as loyalty schemes and home banking.

It is anticipated that eventually all plastic cards will be chip cards and clearly, in addition to the services mentioned earlier, a facility will be made available to both access and make payments through the Internet.

Visa are currently piloting chip-based technology that stores money electronically and that can be used for low value purchases (under £5.00). The retailers will need a new type of terminal for the transactions, but since the amount is initially so low, it is unlikely to affect hotels for a number of years.

Foreign exchange

Large hotels with a high proportion of overseas visitors will make a contribution to their annual profit by offering foreign exchange facilities to their guests. The service is offered on a one-way basis only: the hotel may sell sterling for a foreign currency. If a guest wishes to buy foreign currency then they have to use a bank. There is no legislation about exchange rates, so the hotel is free to offer whatever price it wishes. This is always lower than the bank exchange rate so that the hotel will make a profit on each transaction. If the bank is charging $1.52 for £1.00 then the hotel might charge $1.55. Rates are usually presented in two ways so that the guests can easily calculate the amount due to them and the price they are paying (Fig. 7.9, overleaf). The customers can see the rate they have to pay to purchase pounds. At the same time they are told the amount they will receive for a round amount of their own currency. Exchange rates for major currencies are displayed in the reception area, or cashier's office (Fig. 7.9).

Hotels will only change notes, because coins will be too costly to transport and handle. A few hotels will follow the convention of the banks and issue a receipt quoting each transaction, the guest's room number, and the exchange rate. This has two advantages: if an error is made, the guest can be re-contacted; and as all exchange transactions are recorded, it is easy to balance the amount of foreign currency to be paid in, and thus to eliminate the risk of fraud by the

		£		£
Austria	(Schillings)	19.95	100	5.01
Belgium	(Francs)	58.58	100	1.71
France	(Francs)	9.54	100	10.48
Germany	(Marks)	2.83	10	3.53
Ireland	(Punts)	1.06	10	9.43
Italy	(Lira)	2788.00	10000	3.59
Japan	(Yen)	182.50	1000	5.48
Netherlands	(Guilders)	3.18	10	3.14
Spain	(Pesetas)	238.25	1000	4.20
Switzerland	(Francs)	2.33	10	4.29
US	(Dollars)	1.55	10	6.45

Fig. 7.9 *Exchange rates.*

operating cashier. Hotel security staff often check against fraud by carrying out spot checks, and making test exchanges with marked currency.

Hotels which operate a computerised system frequently incorporate the updated exchange rates within the front office program. This facilitates the more complex transactions such as part-payment of account in foreign currency, and lessens the likelihood of errors occurring.

Petty cash and paid outs

Petty cash

Taxi fares, laundry and dry cleaning, and other small items are often paid by the cashier's department from a separate petty cash float. This float is reimbursed daily by the hotel's income and individual petty cash vouchers are allowed against the day's takings (Fig. 7.10). It is important for the control of the petty cash float that only authorised payments are made against receipts for the amount spent. Petty cash payments are subject to an upper limit, and are only paid out after being countersigned by a member of the management.

Visitors' paid out (VPO)

This is a payment made on behalf of the guest, and is usually done by prior arrangement which ensures that the client has in fact ordered the payment to be made. For example, a guest may authorise the cashier to pay out a sum of money for an airline ticket that is being delivered to the hotel. Disbursements are also subject to an upper limit as a guard against fraud, and they are not allowed to be posted onto the bills of chance guests. When posting VPOs it

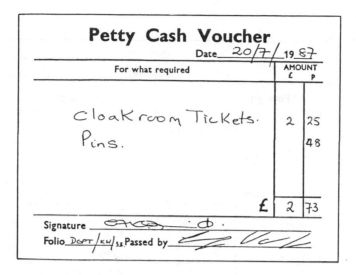

Fig. 7.10 *A petty cash voucher.*

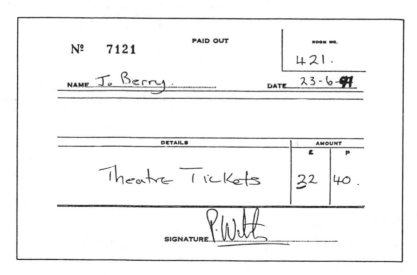

Fig. 7.11 *A VPO or guest disbursement.*

should be remembered that they are exempt of VAT. Whenever possible a VPO, like a petty cash voucher, should be accompanied by a receipt. It should then be signed by the guest or the person receiving the money, posted onto the guest's account and then either placed in the cashier's float to be exchanged for cash or paid into management at the end of the shift (Fig. 7.11).

Department _____			Date _____
			Shift _____
			Cashier _____

Foreign			**Sterling**		
Amount	Currency	Sterling Equivalent	Amount		
	U.S. Trav. Chq.			£50	
	U.S. notes			£20	
	Other Trav. Chq.			£10	
	Notes			£ 5	
				£ 1	
				Coin	
				£ Trav. Chq.	
				Personal Chq.	
				Petty Cash	
	Total £			**Total**	
				+ Foreign total	
				Grand total	

Fig. 7.12 *A paying-in slip.*

Banking

Takings should be paid into the bank each day, so that the hotel receives full benefit from its earnings as quickly as possible. The risk of theft is also lessened.

Departments will pay into the cashier's office or to a general cashier in a large hotel. The paying-in of each department will be summarised on an internal paying-in slip which can be checked for control purposes. These paying-in slips are split into two sections, detailing UK and foreign takings (Fig. 7.12). Departmental takings are then consolidated for paying into the bank.

A paying-in book is used to record the amount banked each day. The book is usually duplicate, one copy being paid in with the banking, and the other remaining in the book for control purposes. Cash is sorted into denominations

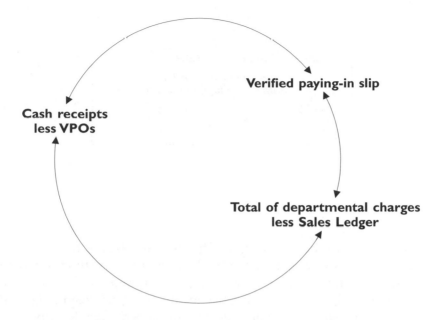

Verified paying-in slip

**Cash receipts
less VPOs**

**Total of departmental charges
less Sales Ledger**

Fig. 7.13 *Circle of control of income.*

and currencies. Coins are bagged, and notes are sorted so that they all face the same way. This 'facing' speeds paying-in at the bank. All banking is entered into the paying-in book. Cheques are listed individually, with the name of the drawer and the amount. A separate page is used for foreign currency, and another page for bank credit cards. Foreign currency is calculated at the current exchange rate, and the surplus is often transferred to a foreign exchange account. Group hotels will use a triplicate book, and send one copy of the stamped paying-in book to head office to enable central co-ordination of income to be carried out.

The amount of money banked each day is the final link in the circle of control that should operate in a hotel. Because the amount banked is verified by an external source (the bank cashier), it completes the checking procedure. This is shown in Fig. 7.13, which outlines the way in which various sections of the hotel's businesses are brought together. The control office or a member of management will check each day to ensure that the figures agree. If they do not, then an investigation has to be carried out to find the discrepancy.

```
Royal Garden Hotel        1646

LUGGAGE RELEASE RECEIPT

Please hand to Doorman to
obtain your luggage. Thank you.


ROOM No....................
```

Fig. 7.14 *A luggage pass.*

Receipts

Guests who pay by cash or cheque upon departure will be given a receipt by the hotel. The system in use will depend upon the accounting method of the hotel. Manual systems of billing will either use a separate receipt book, or a 'paid' rubber stamp. A receipt book is preferable, for the hotel can keep a tight check on the number of receipts issued and the amount of each one. Receipts normally include the name of the payer and details, the amount received in words and figures, the date and the signature of the cashier.

Some patented systems of receipting automatically prepare a paying-in summary for the cashier and at the same time issue a baggage clearance, or luggage pass, for the hall porter. If this system is not used the luggage pass is usually issued by the cashier as the client settles the account (Fig. 7.14). Chance guests who are asked to pay a deposit will be issued with a receipt in the normal way, and the credit will be raised as the first item on the bill.

Receipts from other departments

The cashier is usually responsible for accepting and recording money taken from other sales points, and may also be responsible for reading and checking the tills.

When money is paid in from another cash-taking area (e.g. bar, restaurant, telephone, etc.) the cash should first be counted and checked against the accompanying slip. A receipt should be issued and given to the member of staff, the money placed in the drawer or till, and the details recorded according to the system in use in the hotel.

Advance deposits and prepayments

Advance deposits and prepayments are particularly important in resort hotels where guests may book a substantial length of time ahead. The system varies slightly from one hotel to another, but usually involves the following tasks:

1 A receipt is made out and sent to the client.
2 The amount of the deposit is recorded in the diary (or the equivalent record).
3 The deposit is recorded in the advance deposit ledger.
4 On arrival (or departure), the guest's account is credited with the deposit.

Some hotels adopt a system of raising a credit bill for the guest by making a cash posting for the amount of the deposit. This is not very satisfactory since the bill will become very untidy, and may easily be lost or mislaid before the guest's arrival.

Advance deposits made with a computerised accounting system usually record the deposit in the advance deposit account, and when the guest checks in, the bill is opened with a credit balance of the amount of the advance deposit. Once the credit is exhausted, the bill carries on showing a ordinary balance.

Pre-authorisation

This method of allowing a guest credit is very simple, both for the hotel and for the customer. The guest's credit card is swiped on arrival, and the credit card company reserves a predetermined amount of money for that particular transaction, so the hotel is assured that it will get its money. If the bill goes over the amount then a new sum must be re-negotiated; if it is less than anticipated the original is invalidated, and a new sum is agreed.

Refunds

Occasionally it may be necessary to refund money to a guest, usually because they have paid in advance and have to leave earlier than planned. The bill will carry a credit balance and the usual way of dealing with this is to obtain a VPO for the amount of the refund and post the VPO to the guest's account, thus reducing the total bill to zero. The guest may be given the cash and asked to sign the voucher, which can then be treated in the usual way.

NAME ____________ MR/MRS

ROOM NUMBER ____________

CARD ☐ ACCESS ☐ VISA ☐ AMEX ☐ DINERS ☐ THF ☐ JCB

NUMBER ☐☐☐☐☐☐☐☐☐☐☐☐☐☐☐☐

EXPIRY DATE ____________

DATE OF DEPARTURE: ____________

Address to which account copy should be sent:
(CAPITALS)

....

....

....

If settling your account by Credit Card we invite you to take advantage of our rapid check-out facility. On departure simply complete the details and place this card with your key at the key drop on the reception desk.

A copy of your account together with your credit card voucher will be sent to you on your day of departure.

I hereby agree that my credit card should be used to settle the full amount of my bill and sent to the stated address.

Signature ....

Fig. 7.15 *A rapid check-out card.*

Rapid/speedy check-out

Many hotels have introduced this facility as an extra service for those clients who want to make a 'quick getaway' on departure.

It is essential to ensure that the client is made aware of the facility, and some hotels leave notification of the service in the room, while others advise guests at the check-in point.

The client may be invited to fill out a card giving permission for the hotel to charge the entire account to the guest's credit card (Fig. 7.15). The card has space for the guest's signature, name, room number and credit card number, or alternatively the cashier may take an imprint of an acceptable credit card. Since the cashier has plenty of time, the normal checks regarding floor limit or lost/stolen cards can be carried out without the degree of urgency associated with the early morning rush.

When the client leaves, they need only to deposit the card in a special box, or in the key drop, and the account is finalised in their absence. The cashier may key in the guest's credit card number with the expiry date, mark the transaction 'guest not present' where the signature should be, and send it through to the credit card company. The hotel will undertake to send a copy of the bill and the credit card voucher to the client.

This facility is even more useful to the guest if the hotel property management system has the ability to display an up-to-date copy of the guest's bill through their computer terminal, broken down into departments so that queries can be made instantly. Some systems also allow the guests to request their bags by keying in their room number and the required collection time. This is then logged at the porter's desk and stored until the appropriate time. The same facility can be extended to allow the guest to check out by swiping their own card once they have viewed and agreed the bill. As above, the hotel would undertake to send a copy bill to the client after departure.

Self-assessment questions

1   What dictates the size of the float?
2   Name six methods of payment.
3   List four functions of a cashier.
4   What is meant by liquidity?
5   What is meant by rapid/speedy check-out and what are the advantages?
6   Show how income is controlled.

Assignment

While you are on duty as the senior receptionist, a chance guest arrives and books a room for six nights. When asked for a credit card she becomes rather difficult, and offers to pay a cash deposit against the first night's accommodation. The cash which she has amounts to a little more than half of the room charge, and so you politely decline the cash, and ask again for a credit card. Eventually she passes a card over to you, and since the booking is for six nights you ring for authorisation. The message that comes back asks you to try to retain the card, and authorisation is refused.

Tasks

1   Explain what you will say to the client.
2   How would you endeavour to retain the card?
3   If the client comes up with a plausible explanation, will you let the room for one night? Give reasons for your decision.
4   Compile a checklist to pass to a trainee for accepting credit card payments.

Statistics and Reports

Business statistics

Statistics are an extremely useful method of identifying how the business is doing. The presentation of information in a standardised form makes comparison and interpretation simpler for management.

It is possible to compare actual performance against projected performance and to make internal comparisons – this year against last year, one shift against another, and so on.

Occupancy

The most common and effective statistic in a hotel is the level of occupancy. Most hotels in the UK derive the bulk of their turnover (and profits) from the sale of accommodation. It is essential that management has an accurate, up-to-date picture of the occupancy of the unit.

Occupancy is usually expressed as a percentage. By using the percentage it is possible to make meaningful comparisons. Income alone, for example, is unreliable, for while a hotel may be taking more than the previous year, there is no allowance for any increases in prices that may have occurred.

There are three normal methods of calculating occupancy:

1 rooms
2 sleeper or bed
3 income

The best way of showing how they differ and how they are calculated is to use the following example:

Hotel 50 single rooms
25 twin rooms
25 double rooms
Total 100
Tariff: £50.00 per person per night

All rooms are let. There is only one person in each room. Each room is let at £40.

Room occupancy

$$\text{Room occupancy} = \frac{\text{rooms sold}}{\text{total rooms}} \times \frac{100}{1} = \frac{100}{100} \times \frac{100}{1}$$

So the room occupancy is 100%. At first glance, the hotel is doing very well.

Sleeper occupancy

$$\text{Sleeper occupancy} = \frac{\text{no. of sleepers}}{\text{total possible sleepers}} \times \frac{100}{1} = \frac{100}{150} \times \frac{100}{1}$$

The sleeper occupancy is only 67%.

The term 'bed occupancy' is sometimes used instead of sleeper occupancy, but confusion can arise through the existence of double beds in the hotel, which although they count as one bed, can sleep two people.

Income occupancy

$$\text{Income occupancy} = \frac{\text{actual income}}{\text{total possible income}} \times \frac{100}{1} = \frac{400}{750} \times \frac{100}{1}$$

The income occupancy is just 53%. This is partly due to the discount on the normal rate, but also reflects the poor letting strategy of having only one person in each room. So, although all the rooms in the hotel are let, it is only earning just over half of its potential.

The method chosen by the hotel to calculate its occupancy level is obviously very important. The most accurate picture is given by the income occupancy figure. This shows clearly that 47% of the hotel's potential income on this particular night is lost. The perishable nature of the hotel's 'product', or 'bed nights', means that there is no opportunity to recoup the revenue lost.

The most important point in understanding the profit potential of the hotel business is the perishable nature of the product. A guest buys a room for a **length of time**. So, tomorrow's guest rents the same room but for a different length of time. Other organisations sharing this perishable element include

- airlines
- train companies
- theatres and cinemas

Statistics are one of the key tools in measuring how a hotel is performing and are vital to management decision-making.

Key room statistics

The key statistics gathered by the rooms department are as follows:

- room occupancy
- double occupancy
- sleeper occupancy
- average rate
- % revenue achieved
- REVPAR
- GOPPAR

These are all ways of measuring the performance of the hotel. Later in the chapter there will be an examination of other statistics and reports.

We can illustrate the different types of room statistics by using a sample hotel. The sample hotel has 100 rooms.

Room occupancy

To calculate room occupancy, express the rooms sold as a percentage of the rooms available:

$$\text{room occupancy} = \frac{85 \text{ rooms sold}}{100 \text{ rooms available}} \times \frac{100}{1} = 85\%$$

Naturally, no allowance is made for rooms 'off' for redecoration or maintenance. This ensures that management is not presented with figures that look better than they really are.

To find the room occupancy over a longer period, the calculation is exactly the same:

$$\text{room occupancy} = \frac{\text{total rooms sold}}{\text{total rooms available}} \times \frac{100}{1}$$

For example, for the 31 days in July:

$$\frac{2480}{3100} \times \frac{100}{1} = 80\%$$

Double occupancy

The sample hotel has the following breakdown of room types:

    50   double
    50   twin

Of the 85 rooms sold, 60 have been sold at the double rate so double occupancy is 60%:

$$\frac{60}{100} \times \frac{100}{1}$$

Sleeper occupancy

Sleeper occupancy is sometimes referred to as guest occupancy. This is a useful statistic for calculating restaurant staffing levels and predicting sales of food and drink.

The earlier example shows that there were 85 rooms sold, 60 of which were sold at the double rate. Only 50 were occupied by two people; the other 10 were charged at the double rate but only occupied by one person. So

No. of rooms	No. of guests	
50 double	× 2	= 100
50 twin	× 2	= 100

The potential *maximum* number of sleepers is 200.

The hotel had

No. of rooms	No. of guests	
50	× 2	= 100
10	× 1	= 10
25	× 1	= 25
85		135

$$\frac{\text{actual sleepers}}{\text{potential sleepers}} \times \frac{100}{1} = \frac{135}{200} \times \frac{100}{1} = 67.5\% \text{ Sleeper Occupancy}$$

Average rate

The average rate shows how much a room is being sold for across the hotel.

To calculate the average rate when, for example, room income is £3400:

$$\frac{\text{room revenue}}{\text{rooms sold}} = \frac{3400}{85} = £40.00$$

Figures are normally expressed **excluding** VAT or local sales tax.

% Revenue achieved

Average rate alone does not give a measure of performance against the potential of the hotel. To do that, many hotels look at the revenue as a percentage of the possible maximum.

In the example hotel, the tariff (excluding VAT and sales tax) is as follows:

Room type	1 Guest	2 Guests
Double	£60.00	£75.00 + VAT
Twin	£55.00	£80.00 + VAT

The potential maximum revenue is

50 Double × £75.00 = £3750
50 Twin   × £80.00 = £4000
                     £7750

The revenue achieved was £3400.

$$\frac{\text{actual revenue}}{\text{potential revenue}} \times \frac{100}{1} = \% \text{ revenue}$$

$$\frac{3400}{7750} \times \frac{100}{1} = 43.87\%$$

The hotel that started out with a respectable 85% occupancy is actually only achieving 43.87% of its maximum potential.

> ### Sold-Room 308 for 8 hours
>
> At Schipol Airport, Amsterdam, there is a hotel exclusively for international transient travellers. It is located 'airside' and so guests do not need to go through immigration and passport control to get to it. The tariff allows the guest to book the room for the number of **hours** they require at any time of the day.
>
> So, a guest may arrive from the US at 0700 hours and be departing for Africa at 1700 hours. They could rent the room for the time they needed rather than waiting until normal check-in at midday. How would a hotel like this record its annual occupancy?

RevPar

Even average rate and percentage revenue achieved do not provide a measure against competitor hotels. For this reason, many hotels now use a combination of average rate and occupancy.

This is referred to as 'Revenue Per Available Room' or RevPar. Another term for this is 'rooms yield'.

RevPar = average rate × occupancy%

For the sample hotel

average rate = £40.00
occupancy = 85%

So, RevPar is £34.00.

This allows comparison to be made with competitor hotels with different tariffs and numbers of rooms.

RevPar for a typical month for competitor hotels in a European city could be as follows:

Hotel	No. of rooms	RevPar(£)
A	200	43.70
B	130	29.92
C	170	25.39
D	105	25.82
E	70	21.15
F	100	34.17
G	165	23.89
H	110	27.23
J	105	26.39
K	100	26.85
L	50	37.14

GopPar

Of course, revenue is only one part of the story. Costs are equally important, and to be profitable the hotelier needs to ensure that there is a gap between the two.

All international chain hotels, and many larger privately owned hotels, prepare their accounts in the same manner. This follows the convention set by an American association and is referred to as the Uniform System of Hotel

Accounts. Here costs and revenue are allocated in the same way so that comparisons can be made between different properties.

Meeting room sales provide an example. Should they be allocated to meeting room hire or banqueting? Where should tea and coffee served to the delegates be allocated, and at what price? GopPar, using this standard system of allocating costs and sales, refers to 'Gross Operating Profit Per Available Room'.

'Gross operating profit' is defined as the profit of the hotel before allocating central charges such as bank interest, depreciation and property taxes.

'Per available room' refers to the total number of rooms available during the period. Rooms off for maintenance for short periods would not be excluded, but a block of rooms set aside for major refurbishment would be.

Both RevPar and GopPar have the advantage that they can be compared even if calculated for different periods and different-sized hotels.

Example

Hotel A: 100 rooms
July accounting period 31 days calendar month
Hotel B: 200 rooms
July accounting period 28 days ending 30th

	Occupancy	Average rate	GOP
A	85	40	45 000
B	75	48	82 000

To calculate RevPar

RevPar = rooms available in period × average rate × occupancy%

So,

	Average rate	Occupancy
A 100 rooms × 31 days = 3100	£40	85
B 200 rooms × 28 days = 5600	£48	75

RevPar A = £34
RevPar B = £36

To calculate GopPar

$$\frac{\text{To calculate GopPar}}{\text{GopPar}} = \frac{\text{Gross operating profit}}{\text{Rooms available}}$$

The gross operating profit is

	GOP	Rooms available
Hotel A	45 000	3100
Hotel B	82 000	5600

GopPar A $\dfrac{45\,000}{3100} = 14.51$

GopPar B $\dfrac{82\,000}{5600} = 14.64$

This shows a clear comparison between the hotels even though they are different sizes, and have different accounting periods in the same month.

Occupancy report

The occupancy figures and other information are presented daily to the management and consolidated on a standard occupancy report. This is either prepared by the late shift on reception, or (in larger hotels) by the night audit staff.

Figure 8.1 shows a typical occupancy report for a large city centre hotel. Room types are shown individually to show how rooms are let and which are the most popular. Discounts and complimentary rooms are listed separately so that management can ensure that all reductions have been authorised and see from what source they come. Occupancy information is presented both in room figures and also as a percentage where possible. The number of reservations for the day is shown as 100% so that cancellations and 'no shows' can be expressed as a percentage of reservations. This assists planning for overbooking levels. Apartment income is cross-checked against the amount posted to guest bills. Out of order (O/O/O) rooms of each type are shown in the report. Occupancy this night last year is a quick guide to show how the hotel is progressing. Special events such as exhibitions, conferences and also public holidays are listed, for they will affect the occupancy level that the hotel has been able to achieve.

Guest statistics

The previous statistics have been concerned with the hotel as a whole, and how successful it is. Another group of statistics that are commonly collected relates to the customers who use the hotel.

Room type	Total rooms	O/O/O	Let	Vacant
Single Twin Double Suite Other				
Total				

Discounts and complimentary

Number of rooms	Rate	Name	Affiliation

Day
Date
Unit

	%
Total rooms	100
O/O/O	
Available	
Vacant	
Let	
Sleepers	
Double occupancy	
Reservations	100
Cancellations	
No shows	

Apartment income
Average room rate £

Occupancy week to date
Occupancy this night last year

Special events ....
....
....

Prepared by_____

Fig. 8.1 *Occupancy report.*

Length of guest stay

The average guest stay will affect a number of decisions in the hotel. These concern mainly staffing levels and rotas, facilities offered, and even the number of towels placed in guest rooms.

There are two ways of calculating the average guest stay: the mean average and the modal average.

$$\text{Mean average guest stay} = \frac{\text{no. of sleeper nights sold}}{\text{no. of guests}}$$

The period used for calculating this is generally one month. Normally the figure will not be an exact number of nights, so many hotels will talk of their average guest stay being 2.65 nights, which, although useful, is not clear.

An alternative to this is to produce a statistic which shows the most common length of stay. Obviously, no guest stays for 2.65 nights.

The table below shows the number of nights spent in a hotel by 200 guests.

Length of stay	No. of guests
1 night	40
2 nights	80
3 nights	30
4 nights	20
5 nights	20
6 nights	10

From this, it can be seen that the most common length of stay is two nights. Eighty guests stayed for two nights. This average is called the 'mode'. It is the most commonly occurring figure in the group. The number of nights stayed can easily be logged from departure cards or paid bills.

With this information, it is also possible to calculate the mean average.

Length of stay	No. of guests	Guest nights (1×2)
1 night	40	40
2 nights	80	160
3 nights	30	90
4 nights	20	80
5 nights	20	100
6 nights	10	60
	200	530

By dividing 200 into 530, the average stay of 2.65 nights is found. So, although the mean average is 2.65 nights, over half the guests stay for two nights or less.

Guest origin

Effective marketing begins with knowledge of the customer. Hotels are able to find out more about their customers by reference to registration details (Fig. 8.2, overleaf).

Hotels which operate a computerised system will ensure that this information is readily available as part of the program. Those hotels which still operate a traditional system will find the information more laborious to collect, but essential to ensure maximum occupancy is obtained.

Nationality of guests can be easily logged and presented every three months as a percentage of total guests. This can also be done for UK guests by area or county. The simplest method is to present the number of guests from each country as a percentage of the total. Greater accuracy is produced by showing the guest nights produced by each group as a percentage of the total. For ease of interpretation, these figures are usually presented in a pie chart (Fig. 8.3, page 167) or a histogram (Fig. 8.4, page 167).

A separate chart can be produced for the regions that UK guests come from, if they constitute a major section of the hotel's business.

This information can be used in the planning of sales campaigns or advertising expenditure, or perhaps in the recruiting of staff with special language skills.

Average expenditure

The amount spent by guests is often calculated. This can only be done effectively where expenditure is posted onto a guest's account. Any purchases in cash will be recorded under chance business of the department concerned.

$$\text{Average expenditure} = \frac{\text{total posted to guest's account}}{\text{no. of guests}}$$

A simple average expenditure figure can become more useful if a further classification is made. This can be expenditure by nationality or by business source (travel agents, businessmen, tour guests, etc.).

The amount spent by different nationalities will probably vary substantially. The information can be presented along with the histogram of nationalities; in this way it is easy to compare the information.

Figure 8.5 (page 168) shows that although Japanese guests are responsible for 14% of guest nights, they produced 25% of the income. Their expenditure was markedly higher than that of UK guests.

			For Office Use
Mkt. Type Persons	SURNAME		Room Number
	FORENAME		Arrival Date
	HOME ADDRESS		No. of Nights
			Rate (£)
	Account to be settled by:	Cash ☐ Voucher ☐ Credit Card ☐	Remarks
	Nationality	Car Reg. Number	
Name	OVERSEAS VISITORS	Signature	
	Passport Number		
Dept. Date	Issued at		Receptionist
	Next destination		

RETURN VISITS

Date	Room	Nts	Rate	

Fig. 8.2   *Registration details as an aid to marketing.*

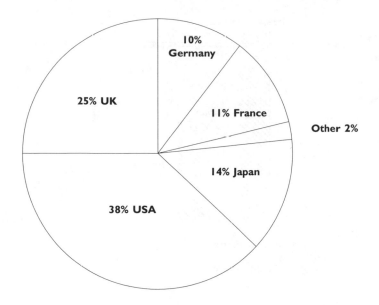

Fig. 8.3   *Pie chart of guest nationality.*

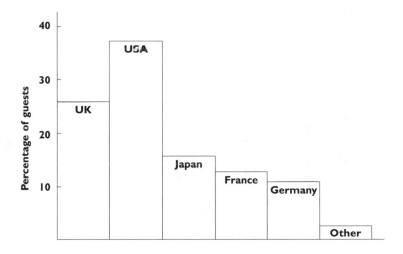

Fig. 8.4   *Histogram of guest nationality.*

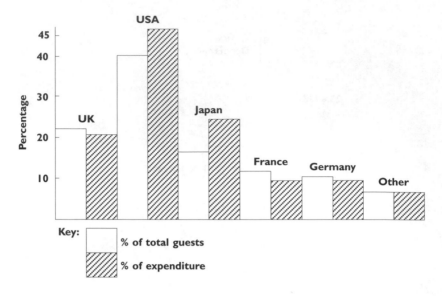

Fig. 8.5   *Guest nationality and expenditure.*

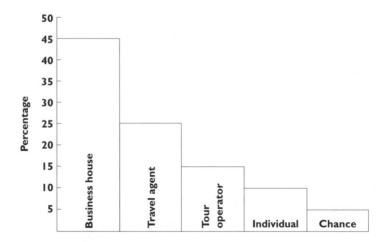

Fig. 8.6   *Sources of bookings in a city centre hotel.*

Source of bookings

The source of bookings can be useful in planning for the hotel. Classification can be either by number of reservations, or by number of room nights. Figure 8.6 shows a profile of a hotel that is mainly business-orientated, and with only a small proportion of package tour guests.

Top 10

With many hotels now operating on a computerised system it is easy to further break down the sources of business. This is often done by producing a list of the Top 10 customers for each segment; for example, the 10 top business houses or the 10 top travel agents.

The information may be presented by showing not only room nights but also total spenditure.

July	Nights	Spend (£)
Abbott Rail	210	13 230
Brown Pharmaceuticals	160	12 000
Creek Telecom	110	6 380
Diamond Insurance	80	4 720
Green University	75	3 675
DRI Hospital	71	5 680
Itochi Computers	64	3 968
Pereira Trading	58	3 886
ABTV	53	2 756
Schnell Freight	49	3 773

By looking at these statistics, the hotel can tell who its biggest customers are. It can also tell what they spend on other services when they are staying. In the chart, DRI Hospital is ranked no. 6. The rooms manager can help the hotel make more money by taking a DRI booking for the last room rather than a Green University or Diamond Insurance booking.

Of course, the risk is that the last room request may not come from DRI and having refused the university, the hotel is left with an empty room. This judgement is what makes the rooms department so interesting. Increasingly though, the experience of the manager is being aided by a yield management system.

Operational reports

A number of reports need to be regularly completed to assist in the smooth running of the hotel. Some of these are completed by the housekeeping department, and checked by reception.

Housekeeper's report

The housekeeping department will send to reception a report on the state of each individual room in the hotel (Fig. 8.7, overleaf). This is generally done twice a day, once during the morning and again at 1800 hours. The reception

4th Floor				Date				19	
401	VAC	421		438		454	VAC	468	
402	OOQ	423		439		455		469	
403		424		440		456⎫		470	
404	OOQ	425		441		457		471.	
406		426		442		461⎭ Suite			
407		427		443		458			
408		428		444		459			
409		429		445		462			
410		430		446		419			
411		431		447					
412		432		449		463			
414		434		450		464			
415		435		451		465			
416		436		452		466			
420		437		453		467			

Housekeeper's Signature

Fig. 8.7 *Housekeeper's report.*

department checks the report against the room status system. Any discrepancies that occur are referred back to the housekeeping department for re-checking.

Accurate completion and checking of the report is very important, especially in large hotels. If the housekeeper's report shows 'vacant' but the room status system shows 'let', it may be that a guest has changed rooms, or even left without settling their account. Failure by the reception staff to follow this up may mean loss of revenue to the hotel. There are many other ways in which the hotel may be losing money, such as only charging one guest when there are two in a room. It is not just the completion of the housekeeper's report that is important, but equally necessary is the checking of all the queries that arise from it.

Incident book/handover book

A log is often kept to ensure the smooth handover from one shift to another. In this, the shift leader will record information and any special incidents that have happened during the day. This is signed by the incoming receptionist. Lost property that has been handed in and passed over to the housekeeper may be noted, or the room numbers of guests who have been requested to pay their bills to date.

Standard room report

The reception department is sometimes involved in the filling out of standard room reports. These are checks that are made periodically on every room in the hotel. The aim of the report is to ensure that the rooms are maintained and decorated to the highest standard. Each part of the room is checked to establish that it is clean, and that all appliances are working. When the report has been completed then maintenance requests are made out as required. A standard room report would check furnishings, wall coverings, lights, directories, curtains, etc., more thoroughly and systematically than would be possible by a maid during her daily shift.

Forecasts

Forecasting is a task of the reception department that affects other areas of the hotel. Restaurants and other sales outlets will base their expectations of trade on the occupancy forecast produced by reception.

Occupancy forecast

A general prediction of occupancy month by month through the year can be made by the reception department. In producing this, its main guidelines will be last year's occupancy, the level of advance bookings already made, and an assessment of any changes in the market. A new hotel opening in the same area may reduce occupancy, while an important trade fair may increase it.

Five-day forecast

A more accurate prediction of occupancy is normally produced by reception for the next five days or so (Fig. 8.8, overleaf). This five-day forecast is done daily, so that the forecast is always updated and extended every 24 hours. It is circulated to relevant departments to aid planning. The forecast will enable the reservations department to accept or reject bookings at short notice and assist the kitchen in buying food for breakfasts and other meals.

Unit _____   Date ☐☐☐

                                 Day ☐

Today   **Departures**

             Overnight vacant   ☐

             + Check out today   ☐

             + Extra departures   ☐

             = Available   ☐

             Arrivals

             Reservations   ☐

             — No shows   ☐

             Net arrivals   ☐

             Vacant (short)   ☐

Day/Date

                              ☐☐   ☐☐   ☐☐   ☐☐

Departures

    Projected check out   ☐   ☐   ☐   ☐

    + Extra departures   ☐   ☐   ☐   ☐

Arrivals

    Reservation count   ☐   ☐   ☐   ☐

    — No shows   ☐   ☐   ☐   ☐

    Net arrivals   ☐   ☐   ☐   ☐

    Vacant (short)   ☐   ☐   ☐   ☐

                              Prepared by _____

Fig. 8.8   *Five-day forecast.*

Financial reports

Sales figures and turnover will be reported daily to management, but some figures may also be presented as ratios or percentages. Management by exception is often practised in the assessment of financial statistics. Upper and lower limits are set by management, and no action is taken unless these limits are exceeded. The limit for bad debts may be 0.7% of turnover. Provided that bad debts do not exceed this figure, no action is taken. This form of presentation is easier to interpret than the raw figures.

Daily trading report

A daily total of sales in every department will be made by the front office. This will show not only the amount spent in each department, but also some measure of activity, such as the number of covers at lunch and dinner. Figure 8.9 shows

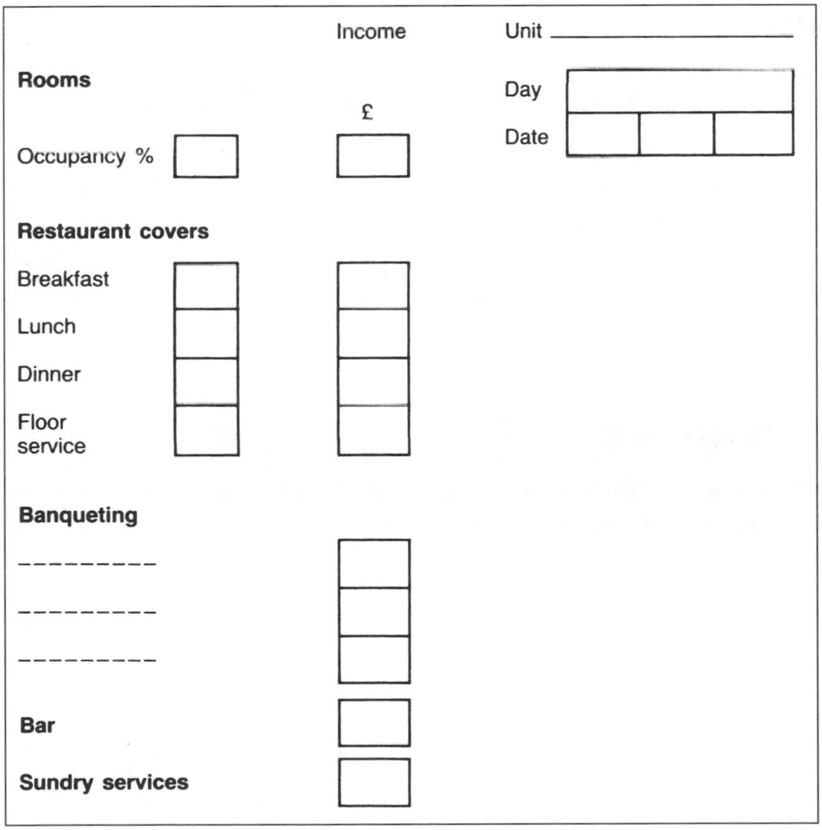

Fig. 8.9   Daily trading report.

a simple daily report of income. If a special promotion is being carried out, then its effectiveness can be monitored by presenting the income of each department as a percentage of total takings. A sales campaign may aim to increase floor service sales from 5% of daily takings to 7%, for example.

Bad debts

Bad debts are normally presented as a percentage of turnover. Included as bad debts would be forged traveller's cheques, as well as the usual non-payment of ledger accounts and 'walk-outs'.

Method of payment

The frequency of the various payment methods can be recorded. The breakdown can be useful in forecasting cash requirements and in preparing cost and sales budgets. Allied to this is the calculation of the length of debt on the sales ledger.

Budgets

Sales and cost budgets are normally prepared by management from information that is gathered individually from each department of the hotel.

The budget system allocates income and expenditure into groups so that profit from each department can be more accurately calculated. Additionally, different hotels which use the system can then compare their operating ratios against each other and against any figures that are published nationally, because every unit that uses the system is calculating its figures and presenting them on the same basis.

Assignment

Design a one-page 'Daily Business Done' report suitable to present to the general manager of a 550-room airport hotel.

CHAPTER 9

Selling Techniques

> **After studying this chapter you should be able to**
>
> - understand the perishable nature of the room as a product
> - explain the different pricing techniques available
> - summarise some key sales techniques
> - complete the assignment at the end of the chapter by preparing a sales plan for a new receptionist

Reception as a sales department

The sales function has become an important and vital part of front office work. With more and more companies entering the hotel and catering field, the public now have a much wider choice, and so it is essential for an establishment to present an attractive and economical product.

The consumer must be persuaded to buy the product and this factor of front office work has influenced the training and selection of reception staff. The receptionist must be capable of making a sale, since front office efficiency is judged on selling success. Sales techniques can be learned, although without doubt some people will have more of a flair for the work.

Although the marketing strategy will usually be devised by senior personnel, it is the reception staff who will implement it. So it is important that front office staff should be aware of the main objectives of marketing a hotel.

Identifying the market

Prior to attempting to sell a product it is important to identify the market. This can be done in a number of ways but many organisations have a section on the registration/reservation card which will assist the management in identifying the sector of the market to which the majority of customers belong.

Hotels frequently have a mixed market which is drawn from both business users and holiday-makers, and each of the market segments may contribute an important part towards the revenue of the hotel.

The most frequently defined market segments are as follows:

1 conference
2 business house
3 independent traveller
4 local travellers
5 overseas holidays
6 domestic travellers
7 government

Identifying customer needs

Once the market has been established, it is then necessary to identify the needs of individual customers. Obviously, those clients who are staying in the hotel for business purposes (probably segments 1–4) will be interested in the service which the hotel provides, may make frequent use of the telephone system, may require the use of a fax machine, or may wish to entertain clients, either in the restaurant or in a suite. Tourists, on the other hand, may be far more concerned with friendly and willing service, since they may be on a limited budget, and use the additional hotel services less frequently.

Marketing mix

It is not impossible for a hotel to capture several sections of the market. It is shown in Chapter 10 that the price offered to a tour operator may well be reduced if the agent is placing a lot of business in the hands of the hotel.

Some establishments are particularly suited to large groups and tours, and find that by letting multiple occupancy rooms they are able to offer a product that fills a particular market. Other hotels may be eager to take their share of the tourist market, but are aware that tours and groups may not fit their image. In a case such as this a special promotion may be offered (e.g. golfing holidays), or a special rate which only applies at weekends.

Whatever strategy a hotel adopts, it is essential to get the right business mix. A hotel that habitually accepts private clients would be very unwise to take a group of low-paying tourists for the same period. Not only do many people feel unsettled by large groups, but it is also unwise to have some clients paying full rack rate when others are staying at a substantial discount. Nonetheless, the hotel is intent upon maximum occupancy and tourist business often provides a welcome source of revenue when the business clients go home for the weekend.

Purpose of selling

Obviously the hotel wants to make a profit every night, but it must also look towards the future, when it will also wish to make a profit. The sales function should really aim to satisfy two basic criteria:

1 maximise the revenue to ensure the best profit;
2 achieve customer satisfaction.

Maximise revenue

Rooms can never be sold twice.

To understand why sales are important in reception it must be realised that hotel rooms, as a saleable commodity, are strictly limited by factors of time and quantity. When selling accommodation, hotels are selling one thing that has two separate parts: accommodation consists of the room itself and a time factor. The customer buys Room 210 on 23rd June, but Room 210 on 24th June is a totally different commodity as far as sales are concerned. This makes hotel rooms similar to theatre or airline seats, where a time element is also involved, in that tickets are sold for the same seats on different days. Figure 9.1 illustrates the point that if the room is not sold on the particular night concerned, then that revenue is lost forever. This characteristic is unlike those of other commodities such as drinks or meals, where the product can be stored until it is requested by the customer. Therefore, for many goods, availability (or production) is more important than selling, but for hotel rooms the reverse is true. Selling is a task of paramount importance because the number of rooms available cannot be affected in the short term to match demand.

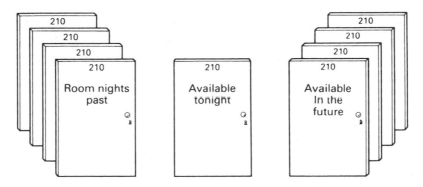

Fig. 9.1 *The relationship between room and time.*

Marginal cost items	Not included
Registration card	Wages of receptionist and maid
Guest bill	
Electricity in guest room	Electricity in public areas
Water heating for bath	
Laundry of linen	TV licence and telephone rental
Soap	Rent and rates

Fig. 9.2 *The marginal cost of a guest room.*

How much profit is there in a room sale?

Economists talk of marginal cost as the cost of producing one more unit of production. In a hotel the unit of production is a room. The marginal cost of a hotel room (Fig. 9.2) is the cost of the items that are used by the guest whilst staying. Not included are those things that would have to be provided or paid for whether or not the room is sold.

Even in a top-class London hotel, the marginal cost of the room is unlikely to exceed £10.00. The difference between the marginal cost and the selling price is the contribution towards fixed costs and profits.

For a restaurant, the marginal cost of a meal or a drink will be a much greater proportion of the selling price. Often the food cost of a meal is 40% of the selling price. Each extra room sale will provide a greater contribution to profits than each extra meal sale.

Another effect of this variation in the marginal cost of a room (against other goods) is the range of prices that can be charged. A room is capable of much greater variation in price with different customers and at different times of the year (Fig. 9.3).

The break-even point and profitability

A result of this low marginal cost is the effect a small change in occupancy has upon profitability. Around the break-even point of sales, a 1% change in occupancy means a 3% change in profits. A hotel that is operating profitably one year can very easily become unprofitable the next, even though the level of business will only have dropped by a small amount. This is clearly shown in Fig. 9.4 (page 180), which also highlights the high fixed costs of operating a hotel.

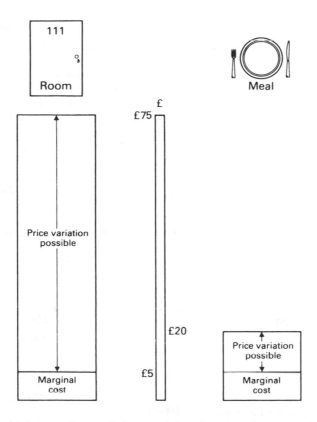

Fig. 9.3 *The relationship between the marginal cost and the selling price of a room and a meal.*

In Fig. 9.4, break-even (the point at which the hotel is covering all of its costs, but not making a profit) is at 65% occupancy.

This rather lengthy explanation of the economics of operating a hotel shows clearly that sales are the most important feature of running a hotel profitably. A manager who spends his or her time on buying, to cut the marginal costs of selling rooms, is not using time effectively, for there is a much greater return in increasing sales, and this should be the area of greatest effort.

Rooms are perishable

Everybody will be familiar with the 'sell-by' date on foods and fresh produce. A room has a sell-by date too. It is tonight. Figure 9.4 showed that each day the room is a different product. This is also true of other 'time-limited' products such as airline seats and theatre performances.

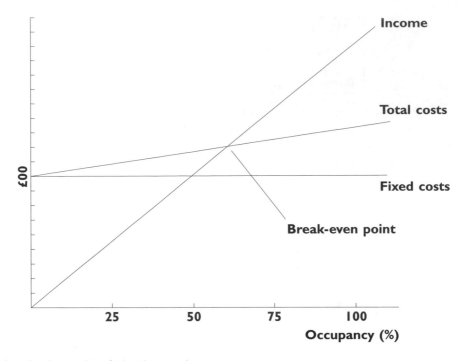

Fig. 9.4 *Break-even chart for hotel room sales.*

GET SOMETHING – ANYTHING

Theatres and airlines approach the sale or surplus capacity very aggressively. In London and in many American cities there is a half-price theatre ticket booth that sells tickets for performances on that night for shows that are not full. Similarly, airlines that have empty seats on a flight offer tickets through 'bucket shops' and other agents at deeply discounted prices.

Of course, the customer trades the lower price for the uncertainty of knowing whether the offer will be available.

Achieving customer satisfaction

There is an old saying about pleasing some of the people some of time, some of the people all of the time, but never all of the people all of the time. Selling is a bit like this.

You may get away with selling an inadequate product or service once, but your customer may never return. Repeat business forms a vital section of the sales function and only by achieving customer satisfaction will you ensure that your customers return.

One hotel director explained this by contrasting the difference between filling a saucepan and filling a colander. No matter how much water you pour into a colander it will never fill. A hotel that loses customers through poor service or a poorly maintained room will never fill, no matter how hard the sales department works.

The hotel product

Selling the facilities to the guest is unique in the opportunity it offers. If the guest is away from home, then it is almost certain that they will want to have a meal and a drink during their stay: intelligent selling by the receptionist will ensure that the hotel's restaurant facilities are promoted fully. A guest who has been travelling for a few days will be delighted to hear of the laundry and dry cleaning service which the hotel offers. The job of the receptionist is to find out the needs of individual guests and suggest ways of satisfying them.

The hotel product could be divided into four main areas:

1 accommodation
2 food
3 drink
4 services

Selling by reception employees involves finding out the needs of customers, converting them into wants, and providing the facilities to fulfil them.

Customer choice

There are several basic reasons why a customer may choose a particular product, and the hotel product is no different to any other.

Need

A customer may buy a hotel room, even if it is not what is really wanted, simply because they need the product. The traveller who is already tired and has driven a long way may feel they need a room so badly that they would pay rather more than usual, or accept something below their normal standards.

Security

Many customers, even those who travel frequently, need the security of staying in familiar surroundings. Hotels which promote a group image provide guests with this type of security, since they can be sure of familiar surroundings whatever country they are staying in.

Comfort

A client may be influenced by comfortable surroundings and subsequently buy the product on view. This is why many hotels take great care to ensure that their front hall facilities are inviting and comfortable, and that their restaurant and bar will immediately put customers at their ease.

Desire

Desire is one of the most common reasons for making a purchase: the customer sees the product and wants it. Many sales are made through impulse buying and for hotels in particular a brochure can influence a potential customer so that they really want to stay in that particular hotel.

Pride

Some customers will purchase a product because they want to be seen owning it. This is particularly true of items like cars where people will pay a great deal of money for a product to be proud of. The same can often be true of hotels – some customers will only stay in an establishment that they can be proud to come back to.

Pleasure

This is one of the best reasons for making a purchase – because it gives you pleasure. Customers of this type are usually very easy to please because they are intent upon enjoying themselves. In a hotel it is particularly important to ensure that your customers' pleasure is not spoiled, and they will continue to stay with you because they enjoy it.

Fear

Fear is a strange reason for buying a product but a common one. People buy an umbrella because they are afraid it might rain. Customers buy hotel rooms even though sometimes it is not what they really want.

A customer may find a room too expensive or not at all to their taste, if but it is 2300 hours and everywhere else is full, the client may well accept the room because they are afraid they will get nothing else.

Fashion

Fashion plays a big part in high street sales, but also makes a contribution to hotel sales. Hotels and restaurants can be 'fashionable' according to who goes there, or the write-up they receive in the press and hotel guides. Many customers want to be seen at the latest 'in' place.

Habit

Many clients will buy the product simply because they always do. This does not mean that a hotel can afford to be complacent; the hotel must ensure that its standards remain as good as ever, and then the customer will continue with the habit.

These are some of the emotional and psychological reasons that may influence hotel choice. Below we look at the more rational ones. The guest will be more aware of these and could quote them as prime reasons if asked.

Location

One of the most important reasons for staying in a hotel is its location. Customers arriving late at night after a long flight will often choose an airport hotel because of its convenient location, even though the city centre may be only 20 km away.

In order to boost sales, a receptionist must be aware of the exact location of the hotel, its access by road and rail, and any other information that may help a prospective client. It is also essential to know the name of the nearest large town if applicable, and any local places of interest.

Facilities

Obviously, a customer will be influenced to make a choice according to the facilities that are on offer at a hotel.

Some clients require little more than cleanliness and pleasant service, while others will require 24-hour service in all departments. The receptionist must know all the facilities that the hotel offers and the prices, if appropriate. The availability of car parking and garage facilities are often of concern to a prospective guest and the front office staff should ensure they are familiar with all sections of the hotel.

Checklists should be compiled for all the other sales outlets and facilities of the hotel. In a large hotel, these are likely to include banqueting, meeting rooms, florist, swimming pool, car hire, sauna, hairdresser, theatre tickets, laundry/valet, kiosk shop, and sports facilities.

With so many facilities and sales outlets, only the most skilled receptionist will know details of all of them without referring to a product factsheet, but every receptionist should know to whom queries should be referred. This is especially necessary for sales leads that may come in for banqueting and conferences.

Value for money

Even the most wealthy of clients still want to see value for money. Most people have no objection to paying for a service, even a fairly expensive one, but they do not like to feel that they have been cheated. If some of your rooms are more expensive than others, explain why. You do not have to be apologetic about price increases, merely ensure that the client is aware of the increase in benefits and services.

Selling methods

A receptionist must be aware of the different skills and techniques required when selling. In general terms, sales can be made in several different ways:

1 personal
2 telephone
3 correspondence
4 fax

Whichever method is in use, many of the basic techniques remain the same. Of all the methods available, face-to-face selling opens up the most opportunity for front office staff to demonstrate their skills.

Personal selling

Selling face to face is a key task for the receptionist. This means actively promoting the facilities of the hotel rather than being passive and merely responding to guests' queries and requests. A personal sales campaign can increase sales of a hotel dramatically, even if it is already trading at a high occupancy.

USP

The first step in personal selling is for the receptionist to develop a unique sales proposition (USP) for the hotel. This is something that occurs only in that particular unit. The product analysis will provide some useful leads which can be compared against the competition in the area. Typical USPs may include any of the following:

• we have a covered garage;
• our night porter will serve food at any time;
• our pool contains fresh water;
• the restaurant is in the *Good Food Guide*;
• all our telephones are direct-dial;
• there is no extra charge for children under the age of twelve.

These USPs should be introduced as a benefit in sales presentation by the receptionist.

Descriptive words

When selling to a potential customer, front office staff should be encouraged to use descriptive words wherever possible. Some attribute of the room should always be mentioned: 'a centrally heated room', 'a twin room with a view of the park', or 'including television with remote controls', etc. All of these things expand the benefits for the guests and help them visualise the room. This use of description must always be followed when talking about the price of a room. A question on price should always be answered with a full explanation of the facilities that the price includes; the price of a room should never be mentioned alone.

Offer alternatives

Professional sales staff always offer alternatives to a prospective customer. To avoid confusion, these should always be limited to two. If a guest requests a double room, the receptionist should reply, 'We can let you have 210, with a private bath, for £60 per night, or 305, which is larger and has a view of the park, for £85.' The guest now has a simple choice between Rooms 210 and 305, and is aware of the extra benefits of the more expensive room. If in response to the request the receptionist simply offers Room 210 at £60 per night, the guest is left to choose between taking it or leaving it. They may well not take the room; even if they do take it, the £25 extra revenue from Room 305 may be lost.

ABC of selling

A simple way of classifying selling by the hotel receptionist is the approach of 'ABC'. This classifies sales into three groups:

- A – automatic
- B – bettered
- C – created

Automatic sales

Automatic sales are the most common form of sale in any hotel. The receptionist is merely acting as an order-taker. The customer knows clearly what is required; all the receptionist does is take the details and fill out the reservation form. Many receptionists never progress beyond this first level of selling.

Bettered sales

Bettered sales are generally described as 'selling up', which is an important method of increasing average rates in hotels. A bettered sale is 'more of the same'. It is a suite instead of a double room, a room with a private bath instead of a room with a shower, etc. Opportunities for a bettered sale may come by intelligent questioning of the guest, or observation, as he or she is checking in. A guest who wishes to stay for a week may take a slightly more expensive room if they are told that it has more wardrobe space. A guest who arrives in an expensive car, but has only booked a single room, may react favourably to the offer of a two-room suite. A skilful receptionist will fit the sale to the prospective guest and learn to identify customers who would appreciate the offer of superior or larger accommodation.

Even the guest who has booked a single room can be told 'Mr Green, since you made your reservation a room with a large bed has become vacant; it is larger and on the side of the hotel that faces the park. Would you prefer that to the room we are holding for you?'

Created sale

The created sale is the sale that the guest did not request, but will accept gratefully. Created sales involve real selling. A created sale is another product entirely. In hotels, created sales would include floor service, dry cleaning, hairdressing, restaurant facilities, sauna – the list is endless. Creative selling in a hotel is relatively easy, for the guest is certain to want to eat. All the receptionist has to do is to show the guest the opportunities that are available. This form of selling must also be fitted to the customer. If a guest checks in at 1100 hours, they should be offered morning coffee, or a booking for lunch in the restaurant. A guest who checks in at 1600 hours may want to have some clothes pressed before going out to a dinner-dance. A guest who arrives late at night can be offered sandwiches and a drink from floor service. A receptionist may be shy of being 'pushy'; creative selling, however, entails satisfying guests' needs and increasing the average expenditure at the hotel. The split of hotel facilities into 'A', 'B' and 'C' class sales is shown in Fig. 9.5.

Return visits

The easiest person to sell to is an existing customer. They know and use the hotel already. Getting a guest to book a return visit is a key part of reception selling. As a guest checks out they should be asked if they are returning again in the future. If the answer is 'yes', then the receptionist can offer to reserve space for them. Many receptionists treat the task of booking return visits as an obstacle race with the guest as the obstacle! Remarks such as 'We are almost

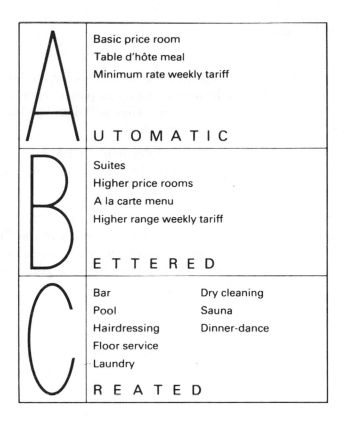

Fig. 9.5 *ABC of hotel sales.*

full then but I will see what I can do' are not designed to make a departing guest feel wanted. Return guests are the lifeblood of a successful hotel and should be encouraged whenever possible.

Telephone sales

Most sales made by telephone in a hotel are from incoming calls. This is the most effort-free form of sales, since the mere fact that the client has called your hotel rather than any other means a choice has already been made. The receptionist should ensure that the client's interest is held, and subsequently converted to a sale.

Basic telephone techniques should be observed to make sure the client receives a good impression of the efficiency of the hotel (see Chapter 3) and the front office staff should ensure that they are well equipped with a product factsheet so that all enquiries can be answered.

Selling by letter/fax

Sales letters

Circular letters are often useful in generating sales leads for the hotel and its facilities. Reception staff should be aware that a campaign is going on, and be fully knowledgeable as to the terms it offers. They will then be able to pass on enquiries to the correct member of management.

A sales letter should follow the traditional salesman's 'AIDA' model in order to be effective. This means that the letter should be arranged in the following way.

A – attention

The beginning of the letter should be designed to gain the attention of the recipient. Not the normal 'Dear Sir, I am writing on behalf of the Grand Hotel to inform you . . .' but something that will make the reader want to carry on, such as 'In this letter there are three ways you can increase your company profits. . . .'

I – interest

The body of the letter should capture the interest of the reader. This is best done by always presenting the material in the form of client benefits. Any letter that carries 'I' or 'we' or 'our' is wrong; it should be 'you' and 'your'.

D – desire

Desire is the next stage of this mnemonic; the customer should be encouraged to find out more, to see the new facilities, to use the bargain break, and so on.

A – action

The final part is action. This converts the interest and desire into a booking or enquiry. Again, it should not be 'If I can help you in any way, please telephone my secretary for an appointment.' Some companies issue a challenge to stimulate action on the part of the potential customer. A very successful sales campaign was based on the challenge, 'If we do not answer the phone before five rings, then hang up and call the opposition.'

Regardless of the medium that is used, most sales begin with an initial enquiry, or a tentative offer. This is your opportunity to open the sale. You may begin by offering a room for the period in question, and quoting the price. If handled correctly, the client's interest will be retained and you may then go on to develop the sale. This gives you the chance to describe the room and its facilities, and stress the value of the room for the price. You may decide at this point to show the customer the room if they are hesitant, and take the opportunity to point out all the good points of the hotel as you go.

Once the guest is sold on the product it is time for your to close the sale. Get a commitment, or even better, a deposit or prepayment.

Handling objections

Every experienced receptionist will be aware of the objections that are used when an attempt is made to sell something to a guest. 'It is too expensive' is probably the most common response. A fully trained receptionist will not be put off by an objection; instead they will have developed individual strategies to overcome the most common objections in their unit. It is only an amateur who is put off by the first objection that a prospective guest raises; the skilled receptionist will handle the objection and still try and sell the facilities of the hotel to the customer.

Assignment

Prepare a sales training plan for a new receptionist who is joining your 50-room country house hotel with leisure facilities. They have no previous practical experience and graduated from hotel school last month.

CHAPTER 10

Distribution Channels and Sales in Modern Hotels

At the end of this chapter you should be able to

- understand how a hotel can use different methods to let potential customers know what it has to offer
- contrast the strengths and weaknesses of each method
- explain how they contribute to the total market for an individual hotel

Distribution channels

Before the guest arrives at a hotel, even before they make a reservation, they have to know the hotel is there. Several hundred years ago, the traditional and only way of doing this was by a sign outside the premises. These early inn signs and 'rooms to let' notices were put up in towns and along highways.

In today's world things are different. There has been a great increase in travel, both business and leisure, nationally and internationally. Transport systems have also developed. Only 100 years ago, the main transport systems were rail and sea. International travel was limited to a very small rich class and merchants. Now it is quite common for people in their twenties to travel thousands of miles for an annual vacation.

This chapter examines the way hotels now let potential customers know that they are there, what they have to offer and at what price. It is essential in a modern hotel to understand and exploit these various distribution channels in a profitable and cost-effective way.

Tracking

The reservations and reception departments play a vital role in providing management with information. Even in the smallest hotel it will be useful to classify guests, as this will help management decide where to spend their marketing budget. This is called 'tracking'. It allows the hotel to track the effectiveness of advertising and sales efforts.

The simplest division is 'business' and 'leisure', so two hotels may have a pattern that varies as shown in Fig. 10.1.

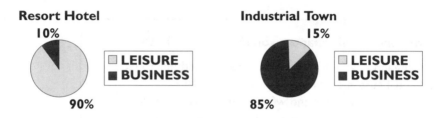

Fig. 10.1 *An example of how guests may be classified into leisure and business guests.*

This, of course, is only the beginning of the picture. What about 'national' and 'foreign'? For an industrial town, the distribution of guests may be as shown in Fig. 10.2.

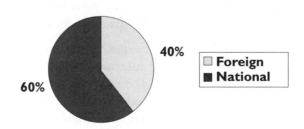

Fig. 10.2 *An example of the proportion of foreign and national guests in an industrial town.*

And now the hotel will want to know what nationalities make up the foreign mix (Fig. 10.3).

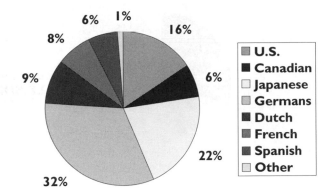

Fig. 10.3   *The foreign guests can also be classified according to their nationality.*

Finally, our targeting for the hotel in an industrial city may look like Fig. 10.4 (overleaf).

These market segments can then be compared against their spending patterns. It may be that for this hotel the pattern is as shown in Fig. 10.5, on page 195.

If the hotel has a choice to make between spending its marketing budget to gain more crew or more delegates, it becomes easier to see which direction to go in.

Dividing the channels

The distribution channels can be split into two main groups:

- controlled
- intermediary

although some media can fall into both categories.

Controlled

The controlled distribution channels are the ones where there is a direct link between the hotel and the customer (Fig. 10.6, page 195). The hotel controls all elements of the message and pays all the costs.

Key controlled distribution channels are as follows:

- newspaper advertisements
- television and cinema
- direct sales team
- central reservations office
- Internet
- strategic partners
- CD-ROM

Intermediary

In intermediary distribution channels there is a link between the hotel and the customer. Sometimes there can be a number of links. However, often the hotel will have no say on how it is presented; it might even be with a competitor hotel (Fig. 10.6, page 195).

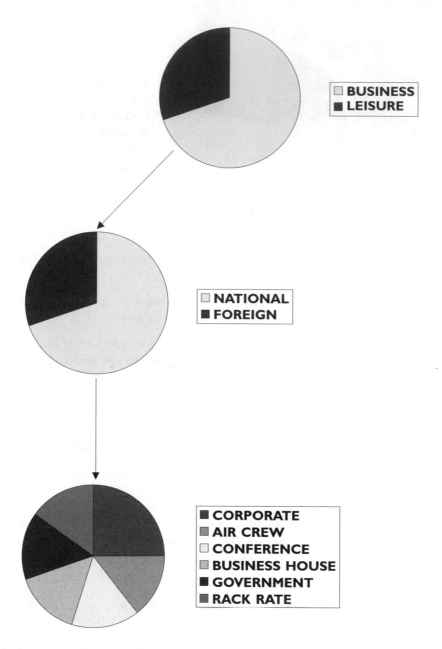

Fig. 10.4   *An example of targeting of a hotel in an industrial city.*

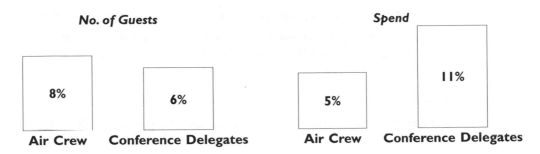

Fig. 10.5 *Market segments can be compared with their spending patterns.*

Fig. 10.6 *Links involved in controlled and intermediary distribution channels.*

Key intermediary distribution channels are as follows:

- tour operators
- conference agents
- travel agents
- business travel agents
- guide books
- Internet
- strategic partners
- CD-ROM

Pricing

These market segments will probably have different rates at the hotel and these rates may vary from month to month. Only the smallest hotels are likely to charge the same price all the time for every room. In setting prices, the key considerations are as follows:

- time of year – which month?
- time of week – which day?
- length of stay – how many nights?
- what is included – breakfast and other meals?
- who they are – regular or one-off?

The reception and reservations department influence the profitability of the hotel by their management of the various distribution channels. An earlier chapter dealt with the concept of yield management. Increasingly this important task is aided by a computerised system which will have cost many thousands of pounds to install. Overall responsibility for this area may well be in the hands of the most senior person in the hotel – the general manager or proprietor. It certainly should not be delegated down to the most recent arrival in reservations.

Packaged rates

Tours will be offered a rate that includes some meals. The package will be built up by the hotel as follows:

Rack tariff		Package cost
£40.00	Room per person	£25.00
£7.00	Breakfast	£5.00
£13.00	Dinner	£11.00
£60.00		£41.00
£10.50	+ VAT	£7.17
£70.50	Total	£48.17

This package rate, often referred to as a '1/2 twin DBB' (one person sharing a double room including **D**inner, **B**ed and **B**reakfast), may be offered to the tour wholesaler at £48.20 with the condition that the minimum group size is 20 people. A further incentive may be one free place for every 25. The wholesaler will 'package' this with the other elements of the holiday, add a profit margin, and offer the tour to potential customers (Fig. 10.7).

These packages are put together by specialist operators between one and two years ahead of the arrival date.

A.	HOTEL ELEMENT × 3 NIGHTS @ 48.20		144.60
B.	HOTEL ELEMENT × 3 NIGHTS @ 39.20		117.60
	COACH TRANSFERS	10.00	10.00
	LUGGAGE HANDLING	1.00	1.00
	ATTRACTION ENTRY		2.80
			276.00
	+ PROFIT 25%		69.00
	= SELLING PRICE		£345.00

Fig. 10.7 *Components of a package.*

Lead times

As the space is booked before the customers have purchased the package there is often a change in the number of guests actually arriving, from the number originally booked. Some tours never arrive at all.

Here the reception has to rely upon a good contract and clearly defined cancellation deadlines. For a hotel that takes tours this could be as follows:

Cancellation within

90 days	no charge
60 days	25% of total bill
30 days	50% of total bill
14 days	75% of total bill
7 days	full payment required

The law of contract plays a part in this. The hotel has a duty to try and re-let the accommodation to 'mitigate loss'.

Contract details will often be printed on the back of the booking form, as shown in Fig. 10.8.

_____ Unit   _____ Date

Tour operator _____   Group name _____

Telephone _____

Telex _____

Contact _____

Rooms	No.	Net rate
SB		
TB		
DB		
Other		

	Arrival	Departure
Date		
Time		
From		
To		

Special requirements_____

_____

_____

Meals		Day of arrival Date ___	Day 2 Date ___	Day 3 Date ___	Day 4 Date ___
	Breakfast				
	Lunch				
	Dinner				
	Function				

Subject to terms and conditions overleaf

Fig. 10.8   _Contract details printed on the back of a booking form._

Handling and billing

The arrival of any group of people together will always place a strain upon the staff of the reception desk. As the reception is aware of the time of arrival of the group and details of the rooms required, the maximum amount of advance preparation can be undertaken.

All departments are notified of the size and arrival details of the tour through the ten-day forecast. When the tour actually arrives, the receptionist should begin by checking the rooming list with the courier to ensure that there have been no late cancellations, or alterations in the room types.

Registration

There are three alternative methods of handling the tour registration. The first is to obtain all details of the group from the operator in advance, and to dispense completely with individual registration cards. This method is quick and cuts down the paperwork. The drawbacks to this method are the lack of confirmation that information provided by the operator is correct, and also the lack of signatures of the individual members; this could cause problems in the verification of charges signed to guest rooms.

The second method is to provide the tour leader with registration cards for each guest, which are completed *en route* to the hotel. As the guests arrive, the cards are handed to the receptionist in exchange for the room key. Key cards will usually have been prepared in advance and will be given out at this stage.

The third method is to register guests in the normal way as they arrive at the hotel. This often causes congestion around the reception desk, to the detriment of other hotel guests, although this can be alleviated by the setting up of a special desk/table just for the tour members.

Room allocation

If the group is large, the allocation of rooms may present some problems. Midday arrival will probably mean that not all of the rooms are ready, so the reception department will have to keep some guests waiting to gain access to their rooms. The allocation of rooms can be organised to place all the tour members as near together as possible. Luggage distribution is simplified by doing this, but an uneven strain may be placed upon one section of the housekeeping department.

The porter's desk will be responsible for providing parking space for the coach, the distribution of mail and messages to the guests, and the speedy distribution of the guests' luggage. On arrival, the bags are carried in, and the total number agreed with the tour leader. Tips may be based upon the number of bags, and the total also acts as a check when bags are brought down on the day of departure. Reception should finally check that a key is available for every room before it is allocated to the new guest.

Guest charges

When booking, the tour operator will have clarified what charges they will be responsible for, and those that the guests will pay themselves.

Charges are posted onto an 'extras' bill for each guest. The bill office staff have to be clearly informed of the breakdown of charges, especially for meals where guests may be charged individually for alcoholic beverages, but coffee and tea may be the responsibility of the tour operator.

The main bill or master account will be charged daily with accommodation and food and beverage charges to ensure that posted charges are a true reflection of the business done on that day.

Check-out

On the day of departure the reception department has to ensure that all extra bills are paid, all keys returned and the baggage cleared before the group departs.

If a tour is leaving later than midday, a hospitality room may be offered to the group. This is a large guest room easily accessible from the lobby of the hotel. Tour guests may use the room to rest, store hand luggage and utilise bathroom facilities before they finally depart. A hospitality room is a courtesy that is much appreciated by tour guests; the hotel also benefits from its use by gaining access to all the guest rooms for servicing by the maids.

The tour leader will give the reception manager a counter-signed voucher itemising all the charges the tour company will be responsible for.

Billing

A copy of the voucher will have been sent to the hotel with the final rooming list. Both of these vouchers are attached to the hotel account, which is completed, checked and authorised by the reception manager and sent to the tour operator for payment. Payment terms are agreed before the tour arrives, for unlike a normal ledger bill, tour bills can often total several thousand pounds in larger hotels. Credit status is checked by the hotel before any bookings are accepted, and also an agreement for handling disputes over the account is established. This will not only minimise bad debt provision but also guard against the tour operator holding up payment of the total bill while a minor dispute is resolved.

Conferences

Conferences, conventions, seminars, exhibitions and workshops are frequently held in hotels that have meeting-room facilities.

The prime purpose for the customer is the meeting itself. The use of bedrooms and food and beverage facilities is of secondary importance. What the organiser is interested in is a package of facilities that will meet all of their needs satisfactorily.

The reception department has to be fully aware of the other facilities of the hotel and their capabilities, if this specialised market is to be met.

Meeting rooms

An accurate plan of every meeting room in the hotel should exist (Figs 10.9– 10.11). The plan must include details of all the mains services and other facilities, but it should be clear enough to be read and understood by a person without architectural training.

The main points in the plan are as follows:

1 full dimensions of the room (including ceiling height)
2 location of entrances and exits, and their size
3 position of dividing doors
4 location of pillars and other obstructions
5 power points and loading
6 gas points and pressure
7 water points and pressure
8 floor type and loading limit
9 lighting and capability
10 air conditioning

The basic information about the room should be supplemented with an inventory of aids to conference presentation. These normally include the following:

1 film projection facilities
2 microphone and amplifiers
3 overhead projectors
4 lecterns and staging
5 slide projectors
6 translation facilities

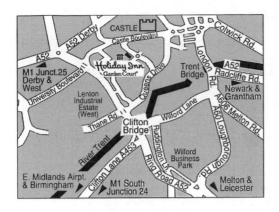

HOLIDAY INN GARDEN COURT

NOTTINGHAM

Castle Marina Park, Nottingham NG7 1GX
Tel: (0115) 993 5000
Fax: (0115) 993 4000

LOCATION/TRANSPORTATION FACTS

- From M1, exit 24, take A453 east. Follow signs for City Centre and turn into Castle Marina. Also access exits 25 & 26.
- East Midlands Airport 20 km.
- Rail station 1.5 km.

ACCOMMODATION

- 4 Floors with 100 guest rooms
- Non-smoking bedrooms
- Facilities for the disabled
- Satelite TV

DINING/ENTERTAINMENT

- "The Conservatory" - intimate bistro-style restaurant. Maximum of 60 covers
- Small friendly bar area adjacent to restaurant

SERVICES/FACILITIES

- Complimentary on-site parking with security cameras
- Bus parking available
- Hertz car rental
- Three other restaurants in immediate vicinity
- Large food superstore across road
- Guest lifts
- Guest voice mail

RECREATIONAL/AMUSEMENT FACILITIES

- Marina adjacent. Castle 1 km.
- "Tales of Robin Hood" Centre 1.5 km.
- Lace Market 2 km.
- "Trip to Jerusalem", claimed to be England's oldest hostelry, 1 km.
- Trent Bridge 2.5 km
- Tennis centre 2 km.
- National Watersports Centre 5 km.
- Sherwood Forest 20 km.
- Jogging trails
- Local tours available
- The American Adventure Theme Park 21 km

MEETING FACILITIES

- 4 Meeting rooms maximum 45 persons
- As executive boardrooms the Clumber Suite accommodates 20 and the Marina Suite 12
- Clumber Suite can be divided into two sections with removable partitioning
- Meeting rooms on ground floor with natural daylight

MEETING EQUIPMENT

(Available by advance request)
- A/V, microphone and sound equipment
- LCD screen for overhead projector
- Lectern. Podium

MEETING SUPPORT SERVICES

- Basic business services of faxing, photocopying, taxi and car bookings
- Flower arrangements
- Assistance with entertainment arrangements

A MEETINGS PLACE HOTEL

Fig. 10.9   *Conference factsheet for a small meeting of 45 delegates.*

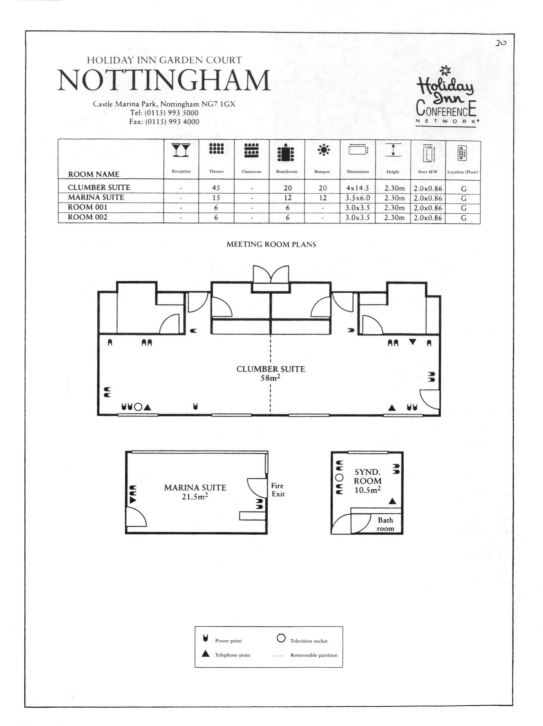

Fig. 10.10   *Reverse side of the factsheet in Fig. 10.9.*

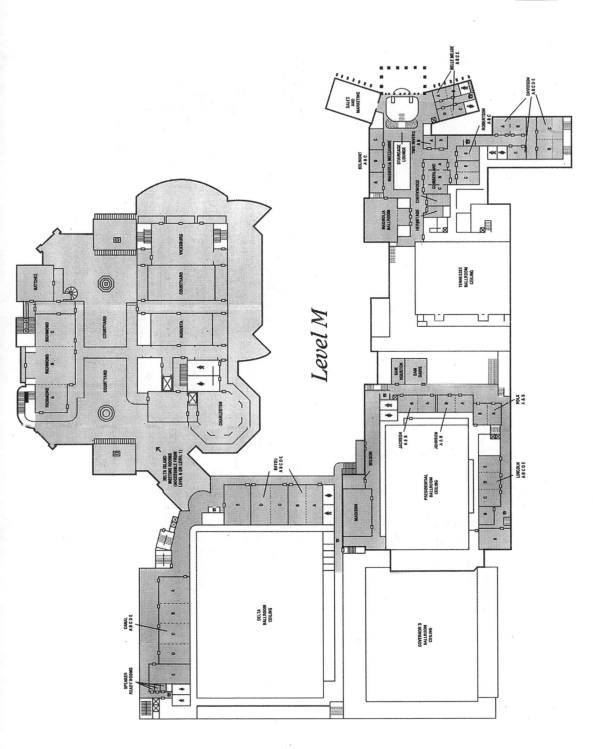

Level M

Fig. 10.11 Conference layout showing 56 000 m² space and a banquet capacity of 5000. (Continued on page 204)

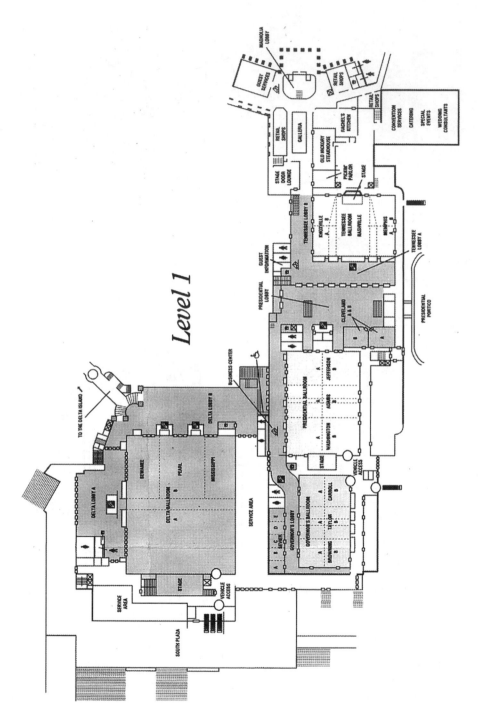

Fig. 10.11 Conference layout showing 56 000 m² space and a banquet capacity of 5000. (Continued from page 203)

Roving microphones and simultaneous translation facilities are only likely to be found in the largest purpose-built conference hotels, but even the smallest hotel will benefit from an inventory of blackboards, flip charts and other equipment.

Seating layouts and plans can also be prepared so that conference organisers may make a choice between the various alternatives; coupled with this should be a knowledge of the capacity of every room in any layout, and advice on the most suitable room for a particular function.

Over a period of time the hotel can build up a folio of photographs of the room in various layouts from previous meetings. These photographs can be a very useful sales aid when meeting conference organisers.

Food and beverage facilities

In selling meeting space, the reception will need to be in close contact with the food and beverage department in order to organise details of meals, snacks and coffee breaks. An effective conference or meeting relies upon accurate timing at all stages and this is essential in the provision of meals. Food and beverage staff are able to assist enormously by serving food swiftly. This may perhaps help conference planners to make up time lost in a session through a seminar overrunning.

Travel agents

Travel agents are as varied in type and size as are hotels. There is the small agent who operates only one local office, but there are also the large international agents such as Thomas Cook and American Express who place millions of bookings a year for all types of businesses from offices in many different towns and countries.

The travel agent will make the booking for the guest and send a confirmation to the hotel. This booking may be only part of a whole series of hotel reservations and travel arrangements that the agent has made for a guest.

Confirmation of the booking is made on a confirmation form which has three copies. One is given to the guest, one sent to the hotel and the third is held by the agent. The travel agent will use this copy of the confirmation to claim commission from the hotel. The commission is a fixed percentage (10%) of the accommodation rate before tax is added. Thus if a guest is booked for three nights in a room at £60 per night, the agent will claim commission of £18 for placing the booking with the hotel.

The agent may take prepayment from the guest, and issue the guest with a voucher that can be used at the hotel (Fig. 10.12). There are three copies of the voucher. On arrival at the hotel the guest gives the voucher to the receptionist

EMPIRE TRAVEL

Bath Road
GLOUCESTER

Voucher No. 123456

Hotel .... Sea View ....

Address .... Park Lane,
London, W.1. ....

Accommodation .... Double with Bath ....

Commencing with ... Dinner ...   On .... 23/06/88 ....

Terminating with ... Breakfast ...   On .... 26/06/87 ....

Including .... Half Board ....

Client name .... Mr & Mrs. H. Jauffret ....

Initials/Ref: *SEJ*

Client (top) copy

Fig. 10.12   *Travel agent's voucher.*

and the amount of the voucher is allowed against the bill of the guest. At the end of the month the hotel will send all the vouchers from each agent back to the agency and the travel agent will pay the total amount owing, minus the commission due.

Hotel booking agents

There are specialist agents who deal only with hotel reservations. The guest contacts the hotel booking agent, who makes the reservation with the hotel and sends the confirmation both to the hotel and the guest. Hotel booking agents often have offices at major rail and air terminals and handle bookings for incoming passengers who do not have hotel reservations.

Commission is also collected from the hotel, but some agents only take commission on the first night's booking, whilst others will claim on the full stay. Bookings which are made by hotel booking agents often have a higher non-arrival rate than normal bookings. Guests who arrive at a booking desk at an airport or railway station may make a booking with a hotel booking agent in case they cannot find an alternative. During the day, they will look around the town and attempt to find a hotel that is more suitable to their needs. If they do obtain alternative accommodation, then only a few will bother to contact the hotel and cancel their booking.

To minimise the problems caused by this, many hotels place all bookings by hotel booking agents on 6 pm release unless prepayment is made.

Alternatively, the agents will charge a booking fee that is the equivalent of their commission.

A booking fee

- increases the arrival %
- cuts down paperwork for both the hotel and the agent
- improves cash flow for the agent

Allocation/allotment

Hotel booking agents and some business houses may negotiate an allocation of rooms at a particular hotel or with a group of hotels. This gives them a guaranteed number of rooms throughout the year; in this way, they can accommodate their regular customers even in periods of high demand. A hotel of 100 rooms may allocate 20 rooms to hotel booking agents and others. This allocation is normally placed on an 'automatic release' basis. If the agent has not made bookings for the rooms by a given date, then they are automatically reclaimed by the hotel. So, if five rooms are allocated to an agent on a seven-day release, and reservations have been made for only three of the rooms, one week before the arrival date the two remaining rooms are automatically released so that the hotel can sell them to ordinary customers. Rooms that are on allocation to an agent are charged at the same rate and in the same way as any other booking.

The allotment of rooms to an agent is beneficial to both parties. The hotel will gain by ensuring that the agent uses the hotel all year round. The agent saves time, for he does not have to contact the hotel to check if space is available, but can sell a room and simply send the confirmation to the hotel. Reception managers often extend the offer of an allocation of rooms to large companies that are regular users of the hotel. Again this is sound commercial sense, for it enables the company to obtain rooms even when the demand for accommodation is very high.

Global distribution systems

In recent years there has been tremendous growth in global distribution systems (GDS). These GDS are mainly owned by the airlines and originated in their ticketing departments. The major operating names of these GDS are:

- GALILEO
- SABRE
- APOLLO
- AMADEUS
- WORLDSPAN
- SYSTEM ONE

Together it is estimated that these systems are connected to over 400 000 computer terminals.

> **Your hotel on Sabre**
>
> - Sabre is connected in 54 countries
> - to 20 000 travel agents
> - with 130 000 terminals
> - it handles tickets for 740 airlines
> - and makes over 1.6 billion enquiries
>
> Source: Yeoman & Ingold (1997) *Yield Management,* Cassell, p. 124.

To gain access to these systems the hotel needs to register with each of them and 'load' the availability of rooms onto the computer system so that the customer can purchase their requested room. If the inventory is not 'loaded' and kept stocked up then the potential customer will not be able to purchase. In the same way, a supermarket customer cannot buy a tin of soup if it is in the store room rather than on the shelf.

Chain and consortia hotels will do this through their central booking system.

Inside availability

The term 'inside availability' is used to denote the systems that are connected directly to the hotel companies' computer systems. This is also called seamless connectivity. The GDS terminal has direct access to room inventory in the hotel system. The last room can be booked through the GDS. Systems that are not connected have to be updated. A 100-room hotel that received a last-minute cancellation for five rooms is unlikely to update its GDS availability. With a seamless connection it is done automatically and the vacancy is shown on every terminal around the world.

Central booking offices

Groups of hotels will almost certainly have a central booking office. This handles reservations for all the hotels in the chain. Naturally they are connected by a Freephone or local call number. Some Lodge hotels may not take reservations at all, but transfer all bookings to the central office. They are then entered onto the computer system to await arrival. This cuts down staffing requirements in the hotel and increases the opportunity of 'cross-selling' when one hotel is full.

Central booking offices in the UK	
• Best Western	0181 541 0033
• Forte	0800 404040
• Hilton	0800 8568000
• Holiday Inn	0800 897121
• Marriott	0800 221222
• Toby	0345 665544

Internet/WWW

There has been an explosion in use of the Internet or World Wide Web in recent years. A PC with the relevant software can access 'web sites' around the world. Many of these will be run by hotel companies, attractions and destinations.

The 'search engine' of the computer will call up 'matches' of the key words entered. Many people will be familiar with a first search turning up more than 1000 matches. Hotel companies may overcome this by having a 'Hot Key' registered on various systems which quickly takes an enquirer to a 'Home Page'. This may be, for example, 'GO MARRIOTT', which leads to the home page of Marriott Hotels.

At the basic level a web page is simply another form of advertising – an electronic brochure. The interest will come in building the two-way links that will gather information from customers, and allow them to book rooms.

Booking rooms is the reason why many travel intermediaries offer hotels free listing, or discounted representation. Should the guest access the hotel through this system then the agent will be able to claim commission.

Hotel companies are currently examining the Internet to assess whether or not it could be used to reduce the cost of a booking.

US industry observers estimate the cost of booking by different methods as:

Voice booking to hotel	$10.00
GDS booking	$3.50
Internet booking	$2.00

CD-ROM

Guides and directories are now being marketed on CD-ROM disks that can be accessed via a PC. These can be useful for people who travel a lot, company travel departments and conference organisers.

Major benefits include their compact nature and the facility to use maps and photographs. A hotel can show pictures, room layouts, location maps and other information. This provides the potential guest with far more information than a traditional guide or directory (Figs 10.13–10.15).

The current printed edition of *Hotel & Travel Index* is 50 cm thick and weighs 4 kg. All of that information and more can be presented on one CD-ROM.

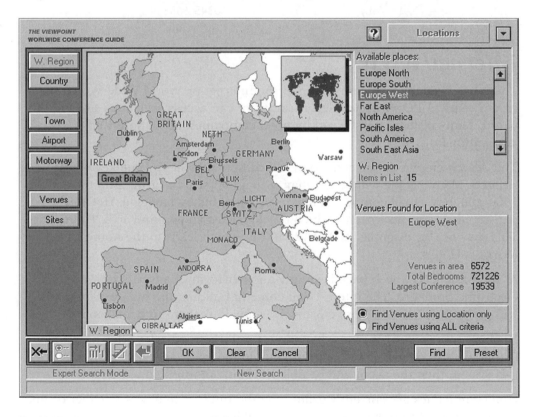

Fig. 10.13 *European location map on a CD-ROM.*

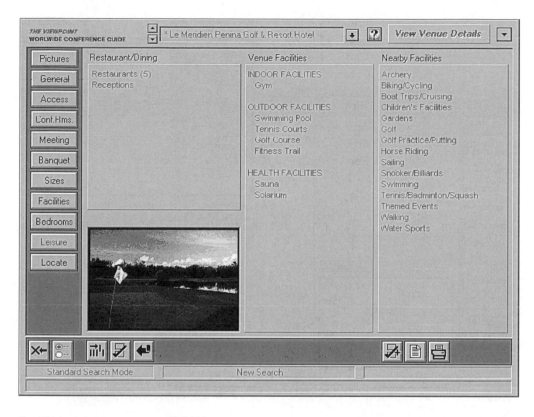

Fig. 10.14 *Leisure screen on a CD-ROM.*

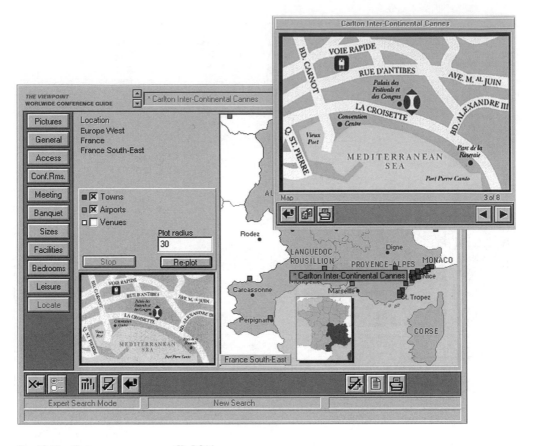

Fig. 10.15 *City access map on a CD-ROM.*

Assignment

Draw up a room plan suitable to include in a sales pack for a meeting room that you have access to.

Index